Tastes Better from Scratch™

COOKBOOK

Tastes Better from Scratch™

COOKBOOK

Easy Recipes for Everyday Life

Lauren Allen

Tastes Better from Scratch

ISBN: 978-0-578-33586-5 (Hardcover)

Printed in China

Food Photography by Lauren Allen and Nicole Leggio.
Lifestyle Photography by Erica and Jon Hayes and Val Dahlin.
Design by LeAnna Weller Smith, Weller Smith Design, LLC.

10 9 8 7 6 5 4 3 2

First Edition

Published by Lauren Allen, Tastes Better from Scratch, LLC.
www.tastesbetterfromscratch.com

Dedication: To my readers, who encouraged me to make this cookbook a reality. Because of you, I get to cook, create, and share my love for cooking every day!

CONTENTS

BREAKFAST

MUFFINS AND BREADS

DINNER

CONTENTS

SOUP

SALADS AND SIDES

DESSERT

INTRODUCTION

On Saturday mornings when I was a child, my twin sister and I were often the first little ones out of bed. With three older brothers, we were the youngest in the family, and nothing sounded more fun to us than digging through Mom's recipe box to choose an exciting breakfast to make all by ourselves.

The kitchen was always a fun and comfortable gathering place in our home. My mom encouraged our help as she prepared food for our family, hosted parties, or delivered food to people in need. I always wanted to be involved, and she helped me learn and let me make mistakes. When I was very young, she let me make simple things all by myself or devise cookie creations with my sister and friends. We made big messes, we were loud, and we had so much fun. When we were teenagers, my friends would gather in Mom's kitchen after school because it was a comfortable, fun space for us to snack and hang out.

Thanks to my family, my love for cooking came easily, and so did my love for trying new foods. I was blessed to travel many places with my parents, and learn about different foods and cultures. My dad's travel expertise ignited a fire in me from a young age that made me want to try every kind of exotic, interesting food. Over the years we had various neighbors and friends that introduced us to more international foods, and we enjoyed making things like spaetzle, spring rolls, and curries at home.

When I arrived at college, it was a bit of a wake-up call to learn that all the great food I was used to didn't exist on campus. It was in the freshman cafeteria brimming with unappetizing food that I came to truly appreciate the value of eating well. Good food is essential for so many reasons, including our physical and financial health and our social well-being. Life's simply too short to eat mediocre food, no matter your budget!

With this realization, I felt a pressing need to compile my favorite family recipes and document the new recipes I was creating. I had decided to

major in journalism, so all of the things I was learning—writing, editing, photography, new media design—came together to help me turn my compilation into a food blog that quickly became my new favorite hobby. I named the compilation "Tastes Better from Scratch," which not only summed up the type of food I had learned to make at home, but also was the most frugal way to cook, making it a good fit for my tiny college budget!

During a semester abroad in Madrid, Spain, I fine-tuned my Spanish and learned even more about cooking from my host mother, the self-proclaimed "best cook in Spain." Not long after, as a newlywed, I was excited to finally have my own private kitchen where I could hone my skills. Having grown up surrounded by great cooks, I was surprised to learn that cooking intimidates some people. I loved sharing recipes with friends and neighbors and offering tips to help them have successful cooking experiences.

My husband and I were able to spend some time living in Mexico, where my happiest memories are of the times we spent with locals who taught us about their food and culture. I soaked up all I was learning and loved experimenting in my own kitchen. As I shared recipes, I was surprised to see others finding and enjoying them, and the blog began to grow like I never expected.

With Jeff, my childhood sweetheart, best friend, and husband.

When I think about why people continue to follow my website, I think it's the fact that I try to share recipes that are fresh, fun, and usually don't require a ton of effort or prep. They're from-scratch gourmet dishes, but without intimidating ingredients or techniques. And most importantly, they're recipes for everyday real life that will work on any budget and for any level of home cook.

Now that I have four young children at home, I hope that their time in the kitchen and at the dinner table will offer the sense of warmth, comfort, and closeness that I felt growing up. Despite how chaotic life can be, making time to eat together and gather around the dinner table as a family will always be a priority for me, and great food is an easy way to enhance that experience.

It all started here, with my sister, Liz, Mom, Colleen, and me, in the kitchen.

This cookbook has been years in the making, and contains dozens of treasured family recipes with decades of testing and trust behind them, along with many of my own creations that have been tested and tweaked countless times. I hope it will serve as a cooking bible that you can turn to for every great recipe you could possibly want or need. I'm so happy I get to share this food with you all—I hope you'll jump right in, roll up your sleeves, and get to cooking something great!

 **Lauren**

HOW TO USE THIS BOOK

As a busy mom of four, I know how hard it can be to get healthy, well-balanced meals on the table night after night. That's why I've included tips and notes throughout this book to help you streamline the cooking process and create delicious, homemade meals for your family on even the busiest of weeknights. Watch for these notes throughout the recipes:

MAKE-AHEAD INSTRUCTIONS: As I'm preparing to cook, I always think about what I can do ahead of time. Many of my recipes have components that can be made in advance, like chopping vegetables, marinating meat, and measuring spices. Getting a head start on a recipe is a great way to streamline the cooking process, leaving more time for enjoying food and family.

FREEZING INSTRUCTIONS: If a dish freezes well, I'll often double the recipe so I have enough on hand for a quick snack or easy meal another day. When ready-made food is in the freezer, you won't be tempted to stop for fast food or turn to prepackaged snacks, saving you money and calories on even your busiest days.

INGREDIENT TIPS AND SUBSTITUTIONS: Where applicable, I've included tips for substituting ingredients to help you make these recipes successfully with what you have on hand. For example, turn to these tips to find out how you can use milk and lemon juice as a substitute for buttermilk, or how to swap in instant yeast in place of active dry yeast.

VARIATIONS: Look for my suggested variations throughout the book for tips on changing up the flavor of a recipe to keep things interesting or to suit your own family's tastes.

 TIP: Finally, you'll notice that some recipes include a QR code. Scan the code using your phone's camera to view a step-by-step video for that recipe.

A FEW TIPS FOR CONFIDENCE IN THE KITCHEN

One of the best ways to enjoy cooking is to be prepared with the right tools, the right ingredients, and a meal plan! Here are some of the basics you'll need to feel confident making each and every one of my recipes.

THE RIGHT TOOLS

CHEF'S KNIFE: A good-quality knife is the best investment you can make. Treat it well. Wash it by hand, and sharpen it often.

PARCHMENT PAPER: I use it to line the pans for all my baking, from quick-bread loaves to cookie bars.

DUTCH OVEN: My Dutch oven was the first expensive kitchen pot I treated myself to, and it has become my right hand! I prefer the enameled pots, which are easy to clean and can be used to cook anything. They're great for everything from sautéing veggies to simmering Panang Curry (page 127) and soups (pages 142 to 161) to stove-to-oven cooking, as for my favorite Braised Short Ribs (page 139).

SILICONE SPATULAS: These are obviously great for stirring batters and folding in ingredients, but I also love them because they withstand heat on the stove, so they can be used to stir hot foods and scrape around the edges of pans without scratching them.

GARLIC PRESS: Fresh garlic is a must, and having a really good garlic press makes it easy.

TONGS: These are my go-to for cooking, flipping, and tossing foods on the stove or the grill.

GRATER: I use a box grater to grate cheeses; shred vegetables, like the potatoes in the Broccoli Cheese Soup on page 147; and grate frozen butter for pastries, like the Perfect Pie Crust on page 225 and the Easy Homemade Scones on page 40.

MICROPLANE: A microplane is ideal for zesting citrus, grating garlic, and shredding Parmesan over spaghetti, pizza, or Classic Italian Lasagna (page 100).

THE RIGHT INGREDIENTS

OLIVE OIL: I use an inexpensive light olive oil for sautéing and cooking at the stove, and a good quality extra-virgin olive oil for garnishing, dipping, and making salad dressings.

SALT AND PEPPER GRINDERS: Cracking these spices yourself adds such great flavor—once you start, you won't be able to go back to preground!

VANILLA EXTRACT: Pure vanilla extract is essential for quality baking. Its rich flavor will elevate your desserts in a way imitation extract can't.

FRESH GARLIC: A bottle of minced garlic may seem convenient, but its flavor pales in comparison to the fresh stuff. I promise you'll elevate your dishes by using fresh—and the aroma in your kitchen will prove it, too!

SPICES AND BAKING LEAVENERS: Spices expire, and if you store them close to the oven or stove, they'll lose their potency even faster. I like to check mine once a year.

BLOCK CHEESES: Always grate cheese yourself! Preshredded cheese from the store contains preservatives to help keep the cheese from sticking together. As a result, it doesn't melt well and doesn't taste as good.

BETTER THAN BOUILLON® PASTE: I always choose this paste over cubed or granulated bouillon because the flavor is richer. I even add a little to my mashed potatoes!

A MEAL PLAN

Having a meal plan in place at the start of each week is the best way to simplify your cooking experience. A meal plan:

SAVES TIME. If you plan ahead, you can usually aim to shop just once a week. Planning ahead also allows you to take advantage of free grocery pickup, if available.

SAVES MONEY. When you create your meal plan each week, take inventory of what you already have. Plan meals that will use up the ingredients and leftovers already in your fridge to save both money and time.

MIXES IT UP. Planning ahead will help you avoid the same-old dinner rut, allowing you to keep meal time delicious and fun.

HELPS YOU GET PREPPED. Now that you have a plan, you'll be able to look at the menu in the morning and do what you can to prep most, if not all, of your dinner ahead of time.

 TIP: Browse tons of suggested meal plans at TastesBetterfromScratch.com, or create your own and then download a free shopping list. Scan the QR code to get started!

A WORD ON PICKY EATERS

I imagine that convincing their kids to eat healthy food is something every parent worries about. When I had my first child, this became a very high priority for me, and now, four kids later, I'm so proud of the way my children eat and I'm excited to share a few things that I've learned. Here are a few of my favorite tips for encouraging kids to eat healthy, well-balanced meals:

MAKE SURE THEY'RE HUNGRY! Limit packaged snacks or cut them out altogether between meals. Instead, offer healthy options first: Put out a veggie tray with hummus or homemade ranch when they get home from school or when they're whining with hunger.

OFFER VARIETY. Try to cook something different every night. The more opportunities kids have to try new foods, the more willing they will be, because they'll see it as normal and fun, not scary or forced. Having a meal plan for each week will help you ensure variety.

NO SHORT-ORDER COOKING! When I was growing up, my mom would say, "I'm not a short-order cook!" Try to avoid making separate meals for kids and adults, and instead, embrace the idea that everyone eats the same thing for dinner. If it helps, disassemble the dinner for younger kids. For example, if you're serving the Chicken Gyros on page 83, you can

that one day they will, and they can try again a different day. Don't give up because they didn't like something the first—or even the tenth—time they tried it. It could take dozens of tries before they decide they like a new food.

SAVE THE BEST FOR LAST. Wait until they eat the healthy stuff before offering the side dishes you know they will eat easily. For example, I hold off on serving things like rolls, garlic bread, and fruit salad until after my kids have eaten the main parts of the meal.

GET THEM INVOLVED! I've found that the more I involve my kids in cooking (just like my mom did with me), the more excited they are about the whole experience. Allowing them to help takes a lot of patience, but hopefully you'll enjoy the time connecting.

separate the pita, chicken, veggies, and sauce on the plate so your kids feel empowered to choose how they want to eat it. I wish restaurants would offer kids smaller portions of what's on the adult menu rather than completely separate kids' menus. I try not to perpetuate the idea that kids shouldn't be expected to eat what we eat.

TRY AND TRY AGAIN. Don't force kids to eat, but don't offer something different, either. What's for dinner is on the plate, and they can choose how much to eat. In my family, we expect our kids to take courtesy bites and try it. If they don't like it, we encourage them kindly

BREAKFAST

Belgian Waffles

Extra light and fluffy Belgian waffles are so easy to make from scratch. Serve them topped with fresh berries, whipped cream, and my Easy Buttermilk Syrup (page 31).

INGREDIENTS

1¾ cups all-purpose flour

1 tablespoon baking powder

½ teaspoon salt

2 large eggs, separated

1¾ cups milk

½ cup vegetable or canola oil

HOW TO FREEZE

Allow waffles to cool completely, then store in a freezer bag for up to 3 months. Rewarm in the waffle iron, toaster, or microwave.

INSTRUCTIONS

1. Preheat a waffle iron.

2. In a large bowl, sift together flour, baking powder, and salt.

3. Separate egg yolks and egg whites into two different mixing bowls.

4. Add milk and oil to the bowl with the yolks and stir to combine. Stir in the dry ingredients.

5. Beat the egg whites with a mixer until stiff peaks form. Gently fold the egg whites into the batter.

6. Working in batches, cook batter in the hot waffle iron until golden and cooked through.

Buttermilk Pancakes

You'll ditch the boxed pancake mix forever after trying these amazing, light and fluffy buttermilk pancakes. They're so easy to make.

INGREDIENTS

2 cups all-purpose flour

2 tablespoons granulated sugar

1½ teaspoons baking powder

¾ teaspoon baking soda

½ teaspoon salt

2 cups buttermilk

2 large eggs, beaten

2 tablespoons melted unsalted
butter

2 tablespoons milk, as needed

INSTRUCTIONS

1. Heat a griddle to 350°F, or heat a large skillet over medium heat. Grease with butter or nonstick cooking spray.

2. Combine flour, sugar, baking powder, baking soda, and salt in a large bowl.

3. Add buttermilk, eggs, and melted butter and mix just until wet and dry ingredients are incorporated. Don't overmix the batter.

4. Add milk a little at a time until batter is still thick, but pourable.

5. Working in batches, use a ¼-cup measuring cup to scoop batter and pour onto greased, hot griddle. Cook pancakes until bubbles appear on the surface, about 1 minute, then flip and cook for 1 to 2 more minutes.

6. Serve warm, with Easy Buttermilk Syrup (page 31).

LAUREN'S TIPS
BUTTERMILK SUBSTITUTE

Place 2 tablespoons white vinegar or lemon juice in a measuring cup, then add enough milk to reach 2 cups.

- - - - - - - - - -

HOW TO FREEZE

Allow to cool completely, then lay pancakes in a single layer on a large baking tray and place in the freezer for 30 minutes. Transfer to a freezer bag and freeze for up to 3 months.

Classic French Toast

My secret trick of adding flour to the French toast batter yields fluffy and rich French Toast that can't be beat! Check out tastesbetterfromscratch.com for many other fun French toast variations.

INGREDIENTS

4 large eggs

⅔ cup milk

¼ cup all-purpose flour

¼ cup granulated sugar

1 teaspoon vanilla extract

1 teaspoon ground cinnamon

¼ teaspoon salt

8 thick slices bread

INSTRUCTIONS

1. Preheat a griddle to 350°F, or heat a skillet over medium heat. Grease well with butter.

2. Combine all ingredients except the bread in a shallow bowl and whisk well to combine, or combine in a blender and then transfer to a shallow bowl.

3. Working in batches, dip each bread slice in batter, dredging it well on both sides, and place on the hot griddle.

4. Cook for a few minutes until the bottom of the bread starts to get golden brown, then flip and cook on the other side until cooked through, 2 to 3 more minutes.

5. Transfer to a plate and serve warm, with Easy Buttermilk Syrup (page 31) and a sprinkle of powdered sugar.

LAUREN'S TIPS

BREAD

Thick slices of days-old bread work great, or use thick-cut cinnamon bread.

- - - - - - - - -

HOW TO FREEZE

Allow French toast to cool completely, then store in a freezer-safe container for up to 3 months. Reheat on the griddle or in the microwave.

Prep Time	Cook Time	Total Time	Yield
5 MINUTES	25 MINUTES	30 MINUTES	SERVES 12

German Pancakes

My Saturday mornings as a child often included a couple batches of German pancakes, and they made it easy to get out of bed in the morning. Plus, you only need six simple ingredients and five minutes to prepare.

INGREDIENTS

5 tablespoons unsalted butter
6 large eggs
1 cup milk
1 cup all-purpose flour
1 teaspoon vanilla extract
Pinch of salt

INSTRUCTIONS

1. Preheat the oven to 425°F. Put butter in an ungreased 9-x-13-inch baking dish and place in the oven as it preheats, just until melted.

2. Combine eggs, milk, flour, vanilla, and salt in a blender and blend until smooth. Pour batter into baking dish, over melted butter.

3. Bake for 22 to 27 minutes, or until edges are golden brown and puffy.

4. Sprinkle powdered sugar over the cooked pancake and cut into 12 squares. Serve with syrup drizzled on top.

Easy Buttermilk Syrup

Basic pantry ingredients and ten minutes is all it takes to make this delicious homemade syrup.

INGREDIENTS

8 tablespoons (1 stick) unsalted butter

½ cup granulated sugar

½ cup packed light brown sugar

1 cup buttermilk

½ teaspoon ground cinnamon

½ teaspoon baking soda

1 tablespoon vanilla extract

STORING LEFTOVERS

Store leftover syrup covered in the refrigerator for up to 3 weeks. Rewarm on the stove or in the microwave.

INSTRUCTIONS

1. Melt butter in a large saucepan over medium heat.

2. Add sugar, brown sugar, buttermilk, and cinnamon and whisk to combine.

3. Bring the mixture to a boil, then immediately lower the heat and simmer for 2 minutes, whisking constantly.

4. Add baking soda and cook for 30 more seconds, whisking constantly. The syrup will begin to foam and rise.

5. Remove pot from the heat and stir in vanilla. Allow to rest for a few minutes before serving.

Really Good

Biscuits and Gravy

Consider yourself warned: Any other biscuits and gravy you try going forward will pale in comparison to this tried-and-true recipe, which my husband's family has been making and perfecting for years.

INGREDIENTS

1 pound pork sausage

2 tablespoons + 1 teaspoon all-purpose flour

1 tablespoon unsalted butter

2½ cups half-and-half

⅛ teaspoon dried thyme

⅛ teaspoon dried crushed rosemary

⅛ teaspoon crushed red pepper flakes *(left out)*

Freshly ground black pepper, to taste

Salt, to taste

Buttermilk Biscuits (page 35), warmed

INSTRUCTIONS

1. Heat a large saucepan over medium heat. Add sausage and cook, stirring and crumbling into small pieces, until browned. Remove most of the grease.

2. Add flour, butter, and half-and-half. Cook over medium-low heat, stirring often, for several minutes until thickened.

3. Add thyme, rosemary, and red pepper flakes. Taste and season with black pepper and salt, if needed.

4. Serve over warm biscuits.

MAKE AHEAD

Make gravy up to 3 days ahead and store in the refrigerator. Rewarm on the stove, adding a splash of half-and-half or milk to thin it, if needed. Taste and add seasoning, if needed.

Buttermilk Biscuits *Excellent!*

These delicious homemade biscuits are folded like a puff pastry, giving them extra layers of tender flakiness. Store-bought biscuits simply can't compete in taste!

INGREDIENTS

2 cups all-purpose flour

2½ teaspoons baking powder

½ teaspoon salt

5 tablespoons unsalted butter, frozen

¾ cup buttermilk

3 tablespoons honey (*leave out if using in a savory dish*)

HOW TO FREEZE

Freeze baked biscuits in a freezer bag for up to 4 months. Thaw at room temperature or in the refrigerator, then rewarm in the microwave.

INSTRUCTIONS

1. Combine flour, baking powder, and salt in a large bowl. Grate frozen butter into the flour mixture. Use a pastry blender or fork to work the butter into the flour. Refrigerate for 10 minutes.

2. Preheat the oven to 400°F. Line a baking sheet with parchment paper.

3. Combine buttermilk and honey in a measuring cup or small bowl and stir to mix.

4. Add buttermilk mixture to flour mixture and stir just until combined and you're able to form a dough ball. Try not to handle the dough too much.

5. Turn dough out onto a lightly floured surface and roll it into a rectangle ½ inch thick.

6. Fold the dough into thirds as if folding a piece of paper to fit into an envelope.

7. Gently reroll dough into a rectangle ½ inch thick. Fold dough into thirds one more time, then roll dough out to a ¾-inch thickness.

8. Cut dough with a 3-inch biscuit or cookie cutter to form about 8 biscuits. Place them 1 inch apart on the prepared baking sheet.

9. Bake for 10 to 14 minutes, or until golden and no longer doughy in the center. *12-14*

Prep Time	Cook Time	Total Time	Yield
10 MINUTES	5 MINUTES	15 MINUTES	4 SLICES

Bacon Tomato Avocado Toast

When it comes to making great avocado toast, quality ingredients matter! Choose the best quality bread, perfectly ripe avocados, and add a touch of fresh lemon and sea salt to make the difference between mediocre and fabulous!

INGREDIENTS

2 large avocados, peeled and pitted

2 teaspoons lemon juice

½ teaspoon sea salt

8 slices bacon

4 large slices of your favorite artisan bread

1½ cups quartered cherry tomatoes

Freshly ground black pepper, to taste

INSTRUCTIONS

1. Combine avocado, lemon juice, and salt in a small bowl and mash until smooth.

2. Chop bacon into small pieces and cook in a skillet over medium heat, stirring often, to desired doneness. Blot out grease with a paper towel.

3. Toast bread.

4. Spread a spoonful of mashed avocado on top of each slice of toast. Sprinkle with a handful of bacon, and a spoonful of chopped tomato. Garnish with fresh pepper on top.

VARIATIONS

Replace the bacon and tomato with any of the following, or mix and match to create your own variation:

FRESH ARUGULA

SLICED TOMATOES, BASIL, AND BALSAMIC REDUCTION

EGGS: Fried, scrambled, or hard-boiled and sliced

SALSA

SMOKED SALMON, THINLY SLICED RED ONION, AND CAPERS

FETA, DICED ONION, AND SLICED TOMATO

Healthy Granola

I've been obsessed with this granola recipe for years and always have it on hand. I love that it's lower in calories and sugar than store-bought, and it only takes a half hour to make a big batch.

INGREDIENTS

4½ cups old-fashioned rolled oats

1 heaping cup unsweetened flaked coconut (I love Bob's Red Mill®)

1 heaping cup sliced raw almonds

½ cup raw sunflower seeds

⅓ cup raw brown sesame seeds (or ground flax seeds)

5 tablespoons unsalted butter or coconut oil

⅓ cup packed light brown sugar

⅓ cup honey

¼ teaspoon salt

1½ teaspoons vanilla extract

¾ teaspoon baking soda

INSTRUCTIONS

1. Preheat the oven to 350°F. Spray a large sheet pan with nonstick cooking spray.

2. Combine oats, coconut, almonds, sunflower seeds, and sesame seeds in a very large bowl and stir to mix.

3. Heat butter in a large saucepan over medium heat. Once melted, add brown sugar, honey, and salt. Bring the mixture to a boil, then immediately remove from the heat. Stir in vanilla and baking soda.

4. Pour immediately over the dry oat mixture and toss to evenly coat. Pour mixture onto the prepared pan and spread into an even layer.

5. Bake for 8 minutes. Remove from the oven and toss mixture, then gently press it down to flatten it back into the pan. Bake for another 8 to 12 minutes, until golden.

6. Allow to cool completely in the pan before stirring or breaking it up.

LAUREN'S TIPS
MIX-IN IDEAS

Replace the almonds with your favorite kind of nuts. Add a pinch of cinnamon for a flavor twist. After baking, add ⅓ cup dried fruit, such as raisins, dried cranberries, or freeze-dried strawberries.

- - - - - - - - -

HOW TO STORE AND FREEZE

Store in an airtight container at room temperature for up to 3 weeks, or freeze for up to 3 months.

Easy Homemade Scones

I can't think of homemade scones without picturing my mom making them on Sunday mornings, and my race against my siblings to grab one warm from the oven. They are irresistible, soft, and flaky, and you can adapt them to add your favorite mix-ins.

INGREDIENTS

2 cups all-purpose flour

⅓ cup granulated sugar

2 teaspoons baking powder

¼ teaspoon baking soda

½ teaspoon salt

8 tablespoons (1 stick) unsalted butter, frozen

⅓ cup plain Greek yogurt or sour cream

⅓ cup heavy whipping cream

1 large egg

1 teaspoon vanilla extract

½ cup dried cranberries or other mix-ins (see Mix-In Ideas, below)

1 cup powdered sugar

1 to 2 tablespoons milk

INSTRUCTIONS

1. Preheat the oven to 400°F. Line a baking sheet with parchment paper.

2. In a mixing bowl, whisk together flour, sugar, baking powder, baking soda, and salt.

3. Grate frozen butter and add to dry mixture. Use a fork or pastry blender to cut in the butter.

4. In a separate bowl, whisk together yogurt, cream, egg, and vanilla until well blended.

5. Add yogurt mixture and dried cranberries to the dry mixture and use a rubber spatula to fold ingredients in until the dough starts to come together in large clumps.

6. Gently knead mixture by hand in the mixing bowl just a few times until it comes together in a ball. Try not to handle the dough too much.

7. Dust a clean surface with a little flour and drop dough on top. Gently pat and shape into an 8-inch circle. Cut into 8 wedges and place on the lined baking sheet.

8. Bake until golden, 16 to 18 minutes.

9. Cool on a wire rack for 10 minutes. Meanwhile, make the glaze: Combine powdered sugar and 1 tablespoon milk in a mixing bowl and stir until smooth. Add additional milk as needed to form a pourable glaze.

10. Once scones have cooled for at least 10 minutes, drizzle glaze over the tops. These are best served the day they are prepared.

HOW TO FREEZE

To freeze unbaked scones, cut prepared dough into wedges and place on a baking sheet. Loosely cover and place in the freezer for 1 hour. Once partially frozen, transfer to a freezer-safe container and freeze for 2 to 3 months. Allow to thaw overnight in the refrigerator before baking as directed. Baked scones can also be frozen for up to 3 months.

LAUREN'S TIPS

MIX-IN IDEAS

Try replacing some or all of the cranberries with chocolate chips, coconut, pecans, raisins, or fresh blueberries.

Prep Time	Cook Time	Total Time	Yield
5 MINUTES	NONE	2 HOURS	1 SERVING

Overnight Oats

The perfect solution to power up your morning that only requires five minutes of prep the night before. Voila! A healthy grab 'n' go breakfast on your way out the door.

INGREDIENTS

½ cup rolled oats

½ cup milk (regular, almond, or soy)

¼ cup plain Greek yogurt

Honey, agave, or maple syrup, to taste

MIX-INS (optional)

½ cup fresh or frozen berries

1 teaspoon chia seeds, hemp seeds, or ground flaxseeds

1 tablespoon peanut butter, almond butter, or other nut butter

2 tablespoons applesauce + 1 pinch ground cinnamon

INSTRUCTIONS

1. Combine oats, milk, yogurt, and honey in a bowl or jar and stir well to combine.

2. Add additional mix-ins, if desired.

3. Refrigerate for at least 2 hours, or up to 5 days.

Breakfast Casserole

Anytime I'm making breakfast for a group, this egg casserole is my go-to, and always gets rave reviews. I love that I can prepare it the night before and pop it in the oven first thing in the morning.

INGREDIENTS

12 eggs

2 cups shredded cheddar cheese

1 cup sour cream (low-fat or regular)

¼ cup milk

½ teaspoon salt

¼ teaspoon freshly ground black pepper

2 pounds pork sausage

4 green onions, chopped

½ green bell pepper, diced

½ red bell pepper, diced

INSTRUCTIONS

1. Preheat the oven to 350°F. Spray a 9-x-13-inch baking dish with cooking spray.

2. Combine eggs, cheese, sour cream, milk, salt, and pepper in a large bowl and mix with an electric mixer on low speed until combined.

3. Heat a large skillet over medium heat. Add sausage and cook, breaking it into small pieces with a wooden spoon, until browned. Drain most of the grease and add the sausage to the bowl with the egg mixture.

4. Return the skillet to the heat, add green onions and bell peppers, and sauté for 2 to 3 minutes. Add to the bowl with the eggs and stir to combine.

5. Pour mixture into the prepared baking dish and bake for 35 to 50 minutes, or until the edges and center are set. (The very center may jiggle just slightly.)

6. Allow to rest for 15 minutes before cutting and serving.

MAKE AHEAD

Prepare casserole as instructed, but before baking, cover with aluminum foil and refrigerate overnight. In the morning, bake as instructed.

- - - - - - - - -

HOW TO FREEZE

Prepare casserole as instructed, but before baking, cover with a double layer of aluminum foil and freeze for up to 3 months. Thaw overnight in the refrigerator, then bake as instructed.

STORING LEFTOVERS

Refrigerate any leftovers and enjoy within 3 to 4 days, reheated in the microwave.

MUFFINS AND BREADS

Healthy Applesauce Oat Muffins

I'm all about healthy muffins that actually taste good, and these ones can't be beat. Enjoy them for breakfast or a healthy snack, or add them to your kids' lunches.

INGREDIENTS

1¼ cups old-fashioned rolled oats

1¼ cups unsweetened applesauce

½ cup milk

1 large egg

4 tablespoons (½ stick) unsalted butter or coconut oil, melted

1 teaspoon vanilla extract

⅓ cup granulated sugar

1 cup whole-wheat flour

1 teaspoon baking powder

¾ teaspoon baking soda

1 teaspoon ground cinnamon

¼ teaspoon salt

½ cup raisins, dried cranberries, or chocolate chips

INSTRUCTIONS

1. Preheat the oven to 375°F. Line a 12-cup muffin tin with liners or grease with nonstick cooking spray.

2. In a medium bowl, stir together oats, applesauce, milk, egg, butter, vanilla, and sugar.

3. In a large bowl, mix the flour, baking powder, baking soda, cinnamon, salt, and raisins.

4. Make a well in the center of the dry ingredients and pour in the applesauce mixture. Stir just until combined; don't overmix.

5. Divide batter evenly among muffin cups. Bake for 15 to 20 minutes or until a toothpick inserted in the center comes out clean. Remove muffins to a wire cooling rack to cool completely.

HOW TO FREEZE

Once cooled, place in a freezer bag and freeze for up to 3 months.

Prep Time	Cook Time	Total Time	Yield
15 MINUTES	25 MINUTES	40 MINUTES	12 MUFFINS

Blueberry Muffins

My favorite blueberry muffins are better than a bakery's and include a delicious cinnamon-and-sugar crumb topping.

INGREDIENTS

2¼ cups all-purpose flour

1 cup granulated sugar

1½ teaspoons baking powder

1 teaspoon baking soda

¾ teaspoon salt

⅔ cup vegetable or canola oil

1 large egg

½ cup buttermilk

1 teaspoon vanilla extract

1 cup blueberries, fresh or frozen

CRUMB TOPPING

3 tablespoons granulated sugar

3 tablespoons packed light brown sugar

3 tablespoons all-purpose flour

3 tablespoons cold unsalted butter, chopped

1 teaspoon ground cinnamon

INSTRUCTIONS

1. Preheat the oven to 375°F. Line a 12-cup muffin tin with liners, or grease well with nonstick cooking spray.

2. In a large mixing bowl, combine flour, sugar, baking powder, baking soda, and salt.

3. Add oil, egg, buttermilk, and vanilla and mix just until combined.

4. Fold in blueberries. Divide batter among muffin cups.

5. To make the crumb topping, combine all ingredients in a medium bowl. Use a fork or pastry blender to cut butter into the mixture. Sprinkle crumb mixture over the top of muffin batter, distributing it evenly among the muffins.

6. Bake for 17 to 20 minutes, or until a toothpick inserted in the center comes out clean or with just a few crumbs.

7. Remove muffins from the oven and allow to cool in the pan for a few minutes before removing to a wire rack to cool completely.

HOW TO FREEZE

Once cooled, place in a freezer bag and freeze for up to 3 months.

Prep Time	**Cook Time**	**Total Time**	**Yield**
15 MINUTES	20 MINUTES	35 MINUTES	12 MUFFINS

Bran Muffins

My mom's bran muffins are the best, most flavorful and moist ones I've ever had. They're loaded with all the good add-ins, and have lots of fiber and protein.

INGREDIENTS

1 cup raisins

1½ cups All-Bran® cereal

1 cup buttermilk

⅔ cup packed light brown sugar

1 egg

1 egg white

⅓ cup vegetable or canola oil

1 tablespoon vanilla extract

1 cup grated carrots

1 cup chopped walnuts (optional)

1 cup all-purpose flour

1 teaspoon baking powder

1 teaspoon baking soda

½ teaspoon salt

INSTRUCTIONS

1. Preheat the oven 375°F. Line a 12-cup muffin tin with paper liners or grease with nonstick cooking spray.

2. Place raisins in a small bowl and add enough hot water to cover. Soak raisins for 10 minutes to allow them to plump. Meanwhile, mix together bran cereal and buttermilk and let stand 5 minutes.

3. Combine brown sugar, egg, egg white, oil, and vanilla in a mixing bowl and mix until combined. Stir in bran mixture. Stir in carrots and walnuts, if using. Drain raisins and discard soaking water; add raisins to the batter.

4. Stir together flour, baking powder, baking soda, and salt, then add to the batter, stirring just until combined.

5. Divide batter among muffin cups, filling them all the way to the top. Bake for 16 to 18 minutes, or until a toothpick inserted in the center comes out clean.

6. Allow to cool for a few minutes in the pan before removing to a wire cooling rack to cool completely.

LAUREN'S TIPS

FOR HIGH ALTITUDE

Add an extra
2 tablespoons flour.

- - - - - - - - -

HOW TO FREEZE

Once cooled, place in a
freezer bag and freeze for up
to 3 months.

Buttermilk Cornbread

My family has been enjoying this cornbread recipe for decades and it always yields perfect, moist, flavorful, sweet cornbread. It makes great cornbread muffins, too.

INGREDIENTS

8 tablespoons (1 stick) unsalted butter, melted

¼ cup white sugar

¼ cup packed light brown sugar

2 eggs

1 cup buttermilk (see note, below)

½ teaspoon baking soda

1 cup cornmeal

1 cup all-purpose flour

½ teaspoon salt

INSTRUCTIONS

1. Preheat the oven to 375°F. Grease an 8-inch square pan.

2. In a mixing bowl, stir melted butter and sugars together until well combined. Add eggs and stir well, until combined.

3. Combine buttermilk with baking soda and stir into the egg mixture.

4. Add cornmeal, flour, and salt and stir until combined. Avoid overmixing—the batter doesn't need to be completely smooth.

5. Pour batter into the prepared pan. Bake for 22 to 30 minutes, or until a toothpick inserted in the center comes out clean.

VARIATION

CORNBREAD MUFFINS: Fill greased muffin cups two-thirds full and bake for 15 to 20 minutes, or until a toothpick inserted into the center of a muffin comes out clean.

LAUREN'S TIPS

BUTTERMILK SUBSTITUTE

Place 1 tablespoon white vinegar or lemon juice in a measuring cup, then add enough milk to reach 1 cup.

- - - - - - - - -

HOW TO FREEZE

Freeze cornbread in an airtight, freezer-safe container for up to 3 months. Thaw in the refrigerator. Rewarm on low heat in the oven, or in the microwave.

Prep Time 10 MINUTES	Cook Time 45 MINUTES	Total Time 55 MINUTES	Yield 2 LOAVES, SERVES 16

Pumpkin Bread

I'm convinced the best way to celebrate the fall season is with a batch of homemade pumpkin bread. This recipe makes two regular loaves—perfect for gifting to friends, or you can freeze the extra loaf to enjoy later.

INGREDIENTS

2 cups granulated sugar

8 tablespoons (1 stick) unsalted butter, softened

3 large eggs

1 (15-ounce) can pumpkin

2 teaspoons vanilla extract

2¾ cups all-purpose flour

1½ teaspoons baking soda

½ teaspoon baking powder

1 teaspoon salt

¾ teaspoon ground cinnamon

¼ teaspoon ground cloves

¼ teaspoon ground nutmeg

½ cup milk

1 (12-ounce) package chocolate chips

INSTRUCTIONS

1. Preheat the oven to 350°F. Line the bottoms of two 8½-x-4½-inch loaf pans with parchment paper and spray all over with nonstick cooking spray.

2. Combine sugar and butter in a mixing bowl and beat with an electric mixer until well combined. Add eggs, pumpkin, and vanilla and mix to combine.

3. In a separate bowl, mix together flour, baking soda, baking powder, salt, cinnamon, cloves, and nutmeg.

4. Alternately add flour mixture then milk to pumpkin mixture, starting and ending with flour. Fold in chocolate chips.

5. Pour the batter into the prepared pans. Bake for 45 to 55 minutes, or until a toothpick inserted in the center comes out clean. (For mini loaves, check them after around 35 minutes.) Cool for a few minutes in the pans before inverting onto a wire rack to cool.

HOW TO FREEZE

Allow bread to cool completely, then place in a freezer bag and freeze for up to 3 months. Thaw overnight in the refrigerator.

Skinny Banana Bread

This recipe has hundreds of five-star reviews on my website—and for good reason! It's lower in calories, sugar, and fat than traditional banana bread, but doesn't sacrifice taste.

INGREDIENTS

4 bananas (about 1⅓ cups)

1 large egg

1 tablespoon vanilla extract

3 tablespoons light brown sugar

2 tablespoons granulated sugar

1 teaspoon ground cinnamon

1½ cups all-purpose flour
   (white or white-whole wheat)

1 teaspoon baking powder

1 teaspoon baking soda

½ teaspoon salt

2 tablespoons unsalted butter,
   melted

INSTRUCTIONS

1. Preheat the over to 350°F. Line two 8½-x-4½-inch loaf pans with parchment paper and spray with nonstick cooking spray.

2. Mash bananas in a mixing bowl. Add egg, vanilla, brown sugar, granulated sugar, and cinnamon and stir well to combine.

3. In a separate small bowl, stir together flour, baking powder, baking soda, and salt. Add to banana mixture and stir to combine. Gently stir in melted butter.

4. Bake for 35 to 45 minutes, or until a toothpick inserted into the center comes out clean.

5. Allow to cool in the pan for 5 to 10 minutes before inverting onto a wire cooling rack.

VARIATION

MUFFINS: Divide batter among the wells of a greased 12-cup muffin tin and bake for 18 to 25 minutes.

Zucchini Bread

My mom's tried-and-tested Zucchini Bread recipe has the perfect blend of spices, a tender crumb, and an amazing flavor. I'm convinced it's the very best zucchini bread!

INGREDIENTS

1 cup granulated sugar

1 cup packed light brown sugar

1 cup vegetable or canola oil

3 large eggs

2 teaspoons vanilla extract

2 cups grated zucchini (grated on the large holes of a box grater)

3 cups all-purpose flour

1 teaspoon baking soda

½ teaspoon baking powder

1 tablespoon ground cinnamon

1 teaspoon salt

¾ cup chopped nuts or chocolate chips (optional)

HOW TO FREEZE

Allow the loaves to cool completely, then wrap in plastic wrap and store in a freezer-safe container for up to 3 months.

INSTRUCTIONS

1. Preheat the oven to 325°F. Line the bottoms of two 8½-x-4½-inch loaf pans with parchment paper and spray well with nonstick cooking spray.

2. In a large bowl, beat together granulated sugar, brown sugar, and oil. Add eggs and vanilla and mix to combine.

3. If zucchini is extra watery, use a paper towel to gently squeeze some of the moisture out. Add to sugar-egg mixture.

4. In a separate bowl, mix together flour, baking soda, baking powder, cinnamon, and salt. Add dry ingredients to the wet ingredients, along with chocolate chip or nuts, if using, and stir to combine.

5. Pour batter into the prepared pans. Bake for 50 to 60 minutes, or until a toothpick inserted in the center of a loaf comes out clean. (If the loaves are browning too much on top during baking, tent a piece of aluminum foil on top until they're finished baking.)

6. Cool in the pans for 10 minutes before removing to a wire cooling rack to cool completely.

VARIATIONS

MUFFINS: Line a 12-cup muffin tin with liners or spray with cooking spray and divide batter evenly among the cups. Bake muffins at 350°F for 20 to 30 minutes.

HEALTHIER ZUCCHINI BREAD: Use half whole-wheat flour, substitute applesauce for half of the oil, and cut out the granulated sugar completely.

CHOCOLATE ZUCCHINI BREAD: Replace ⅓ cup of flour with unsweetened cocoa powder.

Perfect Cinnamon Rolls

Nothing compares to warm cinnamon rolls fresh out of the oven, pillowy soft, swirled in cinnamon, and just begging to be eaten.

DOUGH

2½ teaspoons active dry yeast (see note, page 64)

½ cup warm water

¼ cup + ½ teaspoon granulated sugar, divided

½ cup whole milk, warmed

5 tablespoons + 1 teaspoon unsalted butter, slightly melted

1 large egg, room temperature

1 teaspoon salt

3½ to 4 cups bread flour or all-purpose flour

FILLING

6 tablespoons (¾ stick) melted unsalted butter

⅔ cup packed light brown sugar

2 tablespoons ground cinnamon

¾ cup raisins, chopped walnuts, or pecans (optional)

ICING

4 tablespoons (½ stick) unsalted butter, softened

2 cups powdered sugar

1 teaspoon vanilla extract

3 to 6 tablespoons milk, as needed

INSTRUCTIONS

1. In a small bowl, stir together yeast, warm water, and ½ teaspoon sugar. Set aside for 5 minutes to proof (it should get foamy on top, which shows that the yeast is active).

2. Pour yeast mixture into the bowl of a stand mixer fitted with a dough hook, or a large mixing bowl. Add warm milk, remaining ¼ cup sugar, the melted butter, egg, and salt. Add 2 cups of flour and mix until smooth. Add another cup of flour and mix or knead until combined. Continue kneading the dough for about 5 minutes, adding additional flour if needed to reach a soft dough that pulls away from the sides and bottom of the bowl and is very soft, but not overly sticky. Be careful not to add too much flour.

3. Place dough in a well-greased bowl, cover, and let rise until doubled in volume, about 1½ hours. Meanwhile, butter a glass or metal 9-x-13-inch pan. Set aside.

4. Dust a work surface lightly with flour, or spray with nonstick cooking spray. Punch down the risen dough and transfer to the work surface. Roll out into a 20-x-18-inch rectangle.

continued

FILLING

1. For the filling, spread softened butter over the top of the dough rectangle. Mix brown sugar and cinnamon together, then sprinkle over buttered dough, leaving a ½-inch border. Sprinkle with walnuts, pecans, or raisins, if desired.

2. Beginning on the 18-inch side, roll dough tightly into a log. Pinch the ends together to seal. Use a sharp serrated knife or unflavored floss to cut into 12 equal pieces, each about 1½ inches wide.

3. Arrange rolls on the prepared baking sheet. Lightly spray a piece of plastic wrap with nonstick spray to keep it from sticking, then cover the dough with the plastic wrap. Allow the rolls to rise again for 1 hour.

4. Preheat the oven to 375°F. Uncover risen rolls and bake for 18 to 22 minutes, or until no longer doughy in the center.

5. **MEANWHILE, MAKE THE ICING:** Mix butter and powdered sugar with an electric mixer until smooth. Add vanilla and enough milk to reach a soft frosting consistency. Spread icing over hot cinnamon rolls right from the oven.

Best Homemade Rolls

Is there anything more delicious than light and fluffy homemade rolls? They make the best accompaniment to just about any dinner, and we love them to make sandwiches, too.

INGREDIENTS

⅓ cup warm water

2¼ teaspoons active dry yeast

⅓ cup + ¼ teaspoon granulated sugar, divided

1⅓ cups milk, warmed

5 tablespoons unsalted butter, softened, plus more for brushing tops

1 large egg

1½ teaspoons salt

4 to 4½ cups all-purpose flour

MAKE AHEAD

Make the dough up to 1 day ahead of time, cover well, and refrigerate during the first or second rise. The refrigerator will slow down the rising process.

- - - - - - - - -

HOW TO FREEZE

Baked rolls can be frozen for up to 1 month, stored in a freezer-safe bag or container. Allow them to come to room temperature before eating, or microwave for a few seconds and serve warm.

INSTRUCTIONS

1. Combine warm water, yeast, and ¼ teaspoon sugar in the bowl of an electric stand mixer fitted with a dough hook (or in a large bowl, if you plan on kneading by hand). Allow to rest for 5 minutes, until foamy.

2. Add remaining ⅓ cup sugar, warm milk, butter, egg, and salt. Blend mixture until combined.

3. While mixing on low speed, slowly add 1 cup of flour at a time, mixing until the dough is smooth and elastic, 5 to 6 minutes. You may not need to use all of the flour.

4. The dough should pull away from the sides of the mixer and be soft and just slightly sticky when touched with a clean finger.

5. Grease a large bowl with cooking spray or a tiny bit of oil. Place the dough in the bottom of the bowl and turn it over once to grease all sides. Cover with plastic wrap or a kitchen towel and allow to rise until doubled in size, about 1½ hours.

6. Divide dough into 2 equal portions. Roll each dough ball out on a lightly floured surface into a large rectangle about 11 x 14 inches and ¼ inch thick.

7. Use a pizza cutter or sharp knife to cut the first dough rectangle lengthwise into 2 pieces. Then slice the dough into 6 strips across so you end up with 12 small rectangles.

8. Roll each rectangle up like a snail and place, spiral edge down, on a lightly greased or lined baking sheet. Repeat with the second portion of dough.

9. Cover rolls loosely with plastic wrap and allow to rise again in a warm place until doubled in size, about 1 hour.

10. Preheat the oven to 375°F. Remove plastic wrap and bake rolls for 10 to 13 minutes, until lightly golden. Remove from the oven and brush tops with melted butter.

Easy Artisan Bread

Make a beautiful loaf of artisan bread in your own kitchen with just four simple ingredients—and no kneading! This is the easiest homemade bread you'll ever make!

INGREDIENTS

3 cups all-purpose flour

2 teaspoons coarse sea salt

½ teaspoon active dry yeast
  (or instant yeast)

1½ cups warm water (about 110°F)

INSTRUCTIONS

1. In a large mixing bowl, combine flour, salt, and yeast. Pour in warm water and stir with a wooden spoon until well combined. The dough will be sticky. Cover the bowl and allow dough to rise at room temperature for 4 hours, or in the refrigerator for up to 15 hours.

2. Scoop dough onto a floured work surface and shape into a ball. Sprinkle a tiny bit of flour on top of the dough ball and place it on a piece of parchment paper. Cover the dough lightly with plastic wrap. Allow to rise for 30 minutes.

3. Meanwhile, place an empty cast iron pot, with the lid on, into the oven and preheat oven to 450°F.

4. Remove covering from dough ball. Lift the parchment paper and dough ball up and place both together inside the cast iron pot that's been preheating in the oven. Cover with the lid and return to the oven to bake for 30 minutes.

5. Remove the lid and bake, uncovered, for 12 to 15 more minutes, until golden on top. Remove from the oven and allow bread to cool on a wire cooling rack.

LAUREN'S TIPS

PARCHMENT PAPER

Check to make sure your parchment paper works for high-heat baking.

MIX-IN IDEAS

Add any mix-ins to the flour mixture before adding the water. Try: 3 cloves minced garlic plus 2 tablespoons fresh chopped rosemary, 1 cup of your favorite kind of shredded cheese, or ¾ cup dried cranberries and/or chopped nuts.

NO CAST IRON POT?

Pour 3 cups boiling water into a 9-x-13-inch pan and set it on the lowest oven rack. (This will create steam in the oven to make the bread crusty on the outside.) Place the dough ball on a greased baking sheet and bake for 30 to 35 minutes.

STORING LEFTOVERS

Store bread in an open paper bag on the counter for up to 1 week.

HOW TO FREEZE

Make the dough and place in a freezer-safe bag. Freeze for up to 3 months. Thaw completely in the refrigerator, then allow to rise for 30 to 45 minutes at room temperature before baking. The baked loaf can also be cooled and frozen for up to 3 months.

Pretzels

These fun and delicious homemade pretzels have a salty golden exterior and a soft and chewy center. Don't miss my variation ideas and dipping sauce, below.

INGREDIENTS

2¼ teaspoons active dry yeast (or instant yeast)

1 teaspoon granulated sugar

1 cup warm water

½ cup warm milk

1 tablespoon vegetable or canola oil

1 tablespoon honey

2½ to 3 cups bread flour, divided

1 teaspoon salt

⅓ cup baking soda

4 tablespoons (½ stick) unsalted butter, melted, for topping

Coarse sea salt for topping, if desired

LAUREN'S TIPS

DIPPING SAUCE IDEAS

Cheese Sauce (recipe follows)

Butter, cinnamon, and sugar

Alfredo sauce

Marinara sauce

INSTRUCTIONS

1. Combine yeast, sugar, and warm water in a bowl and gently stir. Set aside for 5 to 10 minutes, until foamy on top. (If using instant yeast, you can skip this step and add everything in step 2.)

2. In a large bowl or the bowl of a stand mixer fitted with a dough hook, combine warm milk, oil, honey, yeast mixture, 1 cup of the flour, and the salt. Mix until combined. Slowly mix in more flour until the dough starts to pull away from the bottom and sides of the bowl, but is still soft. Knead in the mixer or by hand on a lightly floured countertop for 5 minutes.

3. Place dough in a well-greased bowl, cover, and allow to rise for 1½ hours.

4. Preheat the oven to 450°F. Spray two large baking sheets with nonstick cooking spray. Heat 6 cups water in a large pot and bring to a low boil while you shape the pretzels.

5. To shape pretzels, punch dough down and divide into 12 equal portions. Roll each dough ball out into a rope 20 to 22 inches long. To shape into a pretzel, lift both ends of the rope and twist once in toward the center to form a pretzel shape. Set aside on the counter and cover with a towel while you shape the rest of the dough.

6. Add baking soda to the pot with the hot water and stir to dissolve. Working in batches, drop each pretzel into the hot water/baking soda mixture and allow it to soak for 20 to 30 seconds, then transfer to the prepared baking sheets. (I can fit about 6 pretzels on each sheet.)

7. Use a pastry brush to lightly brush the top of each pretzel with melted butter, then sprinkle with coarse salt, if desired.

8. Bake for 8 to 11 minutes, or until golden and cooked through. Store leftovers in an airtight container at room temperature for up to 3 days, or freeze for up to 3 months. Rewarm in the microwave for a few seconds.

continued

VARIATIONS

PRETZEL BITES: Roll dough into an 8-inch rope, then cut into 1½-inch pieces. Dip in soda water as described in step 6, then bake for 8 to 10 minutes.

GARLIC PARMESAN PRETZELS: Remove from the oven 2 to 3 minutes early. Brush with melted butter, sprinkle with freshly grated Parmesan cheese, and return to the oven until cheese is melted.

CHEESE SAUCE:

1 tablespoon unsalted butter

1 tablespoon all-purpose flour

1 cup whole milk, or more as needed

8 ounces freshly grated cheddar cheese (don't use preshredded), room temperature

2 teaspoons hot sauce, or more to taste

Salt and freshly cracked black pepper, to taste

Melt butter in a small saucepan over medium heat. Add flour and cook, stirring well to combine, for 1 to 2 minutes. Slowly whisk in milk and cook until slightly thickened. Remove pan from the heat and stir in cheese a little at a time until smooth. Season with hot sauce and salt and pepper to taste. Add a little more milk to thin, as needed. Keep warm in a small slow cooker or fondue pot. Refrigerate leftovers for up to 4 days. Reheat in the microwave or over low heat on the stove, adding a little milk to thin the sauce, if needed.

Homemade White Bread

Look no further for the perfect loaf of soft and flavorful white bread. With just six simple pantry ingredients, there's almost no excuse not to make homemade bread. It's perfect for making sandwiches, and it freezes well too.

INGREDIENTS

2 cups warm water

1 tablespoon active dry yeast (or instant yeast)

¼ cup granulated sugar or honey, divided

4 to 5½ cups all-purpose or bread flour (see note, right), divided

2 tablespoons canola or vegetable oil

2 teaspoons salt

1 tablespoon unsalted butter, for topping

HOW TO FREEZE

THE DOUGH

Prepare the recipe through step 7, placing the shaped loaves into freezer-safe or disposable aluminum bread pans. Cover tightly with a double layer of aluminum foil and freeze for up to 3 months. When ready to bake, allow the loaves to thaw and let rise at room temperature for about 5 hours, then bake as directed.

BAKED BREAD

Allow baked bread to cool completely. Place each loaf in a freezer bag and freeze for up to 3 months. Thaw at room temperature on the countertop, or overnight in the refrigerator.

INSTRUCTIONS

1. In a large bowl or the bowl of a stand mixer fitted with a dough hook, combine water, yeast, and a pinch of the sugar. Allow to rest for 5 minutes, until foamy. (If using instant yeast, you can skip this step and add everything in step 2.)

2. Add 3 cups flour, remaining scant ¼ cup sugar, the oil, and salt. Mix to combine.

3. Add 1 cup flour and mix to combine. With the mixer running, add more flour ½ cup at a time until the dough begins to pull away from the sides of the bowl. The dough should be smooth and elastic, and should slightly stick to a clean finger, but not be overly sticky. Add a little more flour if needed.

4. Mix the dough for 4 to 5 minutes on medium speed, or knead with your hands on a lightly floured surface for 5 to 8 minutes.

5. Grease a large bowl with oil or cooking spray and place the dough inside, turning to coat. Cover with a dish towel or plastic wrap and allow to rise until doubled in size, about 1½ hours.

6. Spray two 9-x-5-inch bread pans generously with cooking spray on all sides.

7. Punch the dough down well to remove air bubbles. Divide into two equal portions. Shape each ball into a long log and place one in each of the greased loaf pans.

8. Spray two pieces of plastic wrap with cooking spray and lay them gently over the pans. Allow dough to rise again for 45 minutes to 1 hour, or until risen about 1 inch above the tops of the loaf pans. Gently remove the plastic wrap.

9. Preheat the oven to 350°F. Bake for 30 to 33 minutes, or until golden brown on top. Give the top of a loaf a gentle tap; it should sound hollow.

MAKE AHEAD

Make the bread dough through step 4, before the first rise. Place in a large, airtight container and refrigerate for up to 1 day. Remove from the fridge and allow to come to room temperature, then proceed with punching down and forming loaves.

- - - - - - - -

LAUREN'S TIPS

FLOUR

Bread flour or all-purpose flour can both be used with no changes to the recipe. Bread flour will produce a slightly chewier loaf.

QUICK-RISE TIP

To speed up the rising time in step 5, make the dough and place it in a well-greased bowl, turning it once to grease the dough all over. Preheat the oven to 180°F, then turn the oven off. Cover the bowl with a kitchen towel and place into the oven, leaving the oven door slightly cracked open. Allow to rise until doubled, about 30 minutes. Then remove, punch down, and shape into loaves.

10. Invert the loaves onto a wire cooling rack. Brush the tops with butter and allow to cool for at least 10 minutes before slicing.

11. Once cool, store in an airtight container or resealable bag for 2 to 3 days at room temperature, or for up to 5 days in the refrigerator.

DINNER

Black Bean Burgers

Let me tell you what makes these the best black bean burgers you'll ever have: they're packed with bold flavor, they hold together when cooked, and they're unbelievably easy to make. Everyone in my family loves these, and I promise you won't miss the meat!

BURGERS

1 (15-ounce) can black beans, drained and rinsed

½ green bell pepper

½ small onion

2 cloves garlic, peeled

1 tablespoon chili powder

1 teaspoon cumin

Salt and freshly ground black pepper, to taste

1 large egg, beaten

⅔ cup whole-wheat breadcrumbs

CHIPOTLE MAYO SAUCE

1 cup mayonnaise

1 chipotle pepper in adobo sauce, + 1 tablespoon adobo sauce from the can

2 teaspoons lime juice

Salt and freshly ground black pepper, to taste

FOR SERVING

4 hamburger buns

Lettuce, tomato, avocado, onion, etc., for topping

INSTRUCTIONS

1. Preheat a grill to medium-high heat and oil the grates well, preheat the oven to 375°F and lightly oil a baking sheet, or prepare a grill pan to cook burgers on the stovetop.

2. Place black beans in a bowl and blot with a paper towel to remove any extra moisture. Mash well with a fork.

3. Combine bell pepper, onion, and garlic in a food processor and process until finely minced. Transfer mixture to a fine-mesh strainer and press out any excess moisture.

4. Add minced vegetables to the mashed black beans. Add chili powder, cumin, and salt and pepper and stir to combine. Add beaten egg and mix. Stir in breadcrumbs.

5. Form mixture into 4 burger patties.

6. If using a grill or a grill pan on the stove, cook the burgers for 4 to 5 minutes on each side. Or, bake for 10 minutes on each side.

7. Meanwhile, to make the chipotle mayo sauce, combine the mayonnaise, chipotle pepper and adobo sauce, and lime juice in a food processor or blender and puree until smooth. Season with salt and pepper to taste.

8. Serve each burger on a bun topped with a spoonful of sauce and your desired burger toppings.

MAKE AHEAD

Cooked burger patties will keep in the fridge for 3 to 5 days. Rewarm in a skillet over medium heat.

HOW TO FREEZE

Place uncooked burger patties in a freezer bag or airtight container and freeze for up to 3 months. Thaw overnight in the fridge before cooking.

Chicken Salad Croissant Sandwiches

There's a reason this sandwich is so popular to serve to a crowd: it's easy to make, the filling can be made ahead, and everyone loves them. My version has a delicious blend of flavors and the perfect creaminess and crunch to pair with buttery, flaky croissants.

INGREDIENTS

3 cups cooked shredded chicken

3 ribs celery, diced

2 tablespoons chopped red onion

½ cup mayonnaise

¼ to ½ cup plain Greek yogurt, to taste

½ teaspoon Dijon mustard

½ teaspoon salt, plus more to taste

⅛ teaspoon freshly ground black pepper, plus more to taste

½ cup whole cashews or sliced almonds (optional)

1 cup halved grapes (optional)

10 croissants

INSTRUCTIONS

1. Combine chicken, celery, onion, mayo, yogurt, mustard, salt, and pepper in a bowl and mix well to combine.

2. Stir in nuts and grapes, if using.

3. Taste and add more mayo or Greek yogurt and additional salt and pepper as desired.

4. For best results, refrigerate for 1 to 2 hours to allow the flavors to blend.

5. Split the croissants in half and fill each with a heaping spoonful of chicken salad.

MAKE AHEAD

The chicken filling can be made 2 to 3 days in advance, depending on the freshness of the chicken.

Chicken Gyros

These quick and easy chicken gyros are a cinch to whip up, easy to prep ahead of time, and everyone loves them. Just top the Greek-style marinated chicken with simple tzatziki sauce and throw on all the yummy toppings. (Extra feta for me, please.)

MARINATED CHICKEN

2 pounds boneless, skinless chicken breasts or tenders

2 tablespoons olive oil

2 tablespoons lemon juice

2 cloves garlic, minced

2 teaspoons smoked paprika (or regular)

2 teaspoons ground cumin

1 teaspoon ground tumeric

1 teaspoon ground coriander

1 teaspoon salt

¼ teaspoon freshly ground black pepper

¼ teaspoon onion powder

¼ teaspoon ground cinnamon

⅛ teaspoon crushed red pepper flakes, or more to taste

TZATZIKI SAUCE

1 cup plain Greek yogurt

2 cloves garlic, minced

2 tablespoons peeled and finely diced English cucumber

2 teaspoons lemon juice

½ teaspoon dried dill

Salt and freshly ground black pepper, to taste

FOR SERVING

6 pitas or flatbreads

1 romaine heart, finely chopped

1 cup halved cherry tomatoes

¼ red onion, thinly sliced

½ English cucumber, thinly sliced

⅓ cup crumbled feta cheese

INSTRUCTIONS

1. Place chicken in a bowl or resealable bag. Combine all marinade ingredients and pour over chicken, tossing to coat. Refrigerate for 1 to 4 hours.

2. Meanwhile, combine all ingredients for the tzatziki sauce. Taste and add more lemon juice, garlic, salt, pepper, or dill if needed. Refrigerate.

3. Heat a grill to medium and oil the grates, or grease a skillet and place over medium-high heat on the stove. Remove chicken from marinade, letting any excess drip off, and grill for several minutes on each side, flipping once, until cooked through, about 5 minutes. Remove to a plate and let rest before chopping into bite-size pieces.

4. Toast or warm your pitas. Layer cooked chicken, lettuce, tomato, red onion, cucumber, feta, and tzatziki sauce on each pita and serve.

MAKE AHEAD

The marinade and tzatziki sauce can be made 2 to 3 days in advance and stored in the refrigerator.

Italian Meatball Subs

These easy Italian Meatball Subs feature homemade meatballs, baked and topped with a simple Italian marinara sauce on a toasted bun with melted cheese.

MEATBALLS

½ cup crushed saltine crackers

¼ cup low-sodium beef broth

1 large egg, lightly beaten

2 tablespoons dried parsley

2 teaspoons dried oregano

1 teaspoon dried basil

1 teaspoon freshly ground black pepper

½ teaspoon salt

½ teaspoon garlic powder

¼ teaspoon crushed red pepper flakes

1 pound lean ground beef or ground turkey

¾ cup all-purpose flour, for dredging

SAUCE

1 (28-ounce) can crushed tomatoes

1½ teaspoons dried basil

1½ teaspoons dried oregano

1 teaspoon granulated sugar

½ teaspoon garlic salt

SANDWICHES

5 hoagie or sub rolls

10 slices provolone or mozzarella cheese

INSTRUCTIONS

1. For the meatballs, combine crackers, broth, egg, and all the spices in a large mixing bowl and stir well to combine. Set aside for 10 minutes to soften the crackers. Add ground meat and mix just until combined.

2. Preheat the oven to 400°F. Line a baking sheet with parchment paper or foil.

3. Form fifteen golf-ball-size meatballs and gently sprinkle the outsides with flour. Place 1 inch apart on the baking sheet and bake for 20 to 25 minutes, or until cooked through.

4. While the meatballs cook, make the sauce. Combine all sauce ingredients in a saucepan over medium heat. Simmer sauce for 10 to 15 minutes.

5. When the meatballs are finished baking, add them to the sauce. Preheat the broiler.

6. Slice the hoagie rolls in half and layer with cheese. Broil on high for 2 to 3 minutes, or until rolls are toasted and cheese is melted. Remove from the oven and place 3 meatballs on each sub, followed by a large spoonful of sauce. Serve immediately.

MAKE AHEAD

The meatball mixture and sauce can be made up to 1 day in advance, covered well, and stored separately in the fridge.

HOW TO FREEZE

To freeze cooked meatballs, allow them to cool completely after baking, then store them in a freezer bag for up to 3 months. Thaw overnight in the refrigerator and warm in sauce on the stove. Uncooked/raw meatballs can be frozen for up to 3 months. After making the meatballs and assembling them into small balls, store them in a freezer bag. Thaw in the refrigerator before baking as instructed. The sauce can also be frozen for up to 3 months.

Prep Time	Cook Time	Total Time	Yield
5 MINUTES	5 HOURS 5 MINUTES	5 HOURS 10 MINUTES	SERVES 8

French Dip Sandwiches

Picture this: slow cooked, tender roast beef piled on a hoagie roll and toasted with melty cheese on top. You've got yourself a legit French dip sandwich, ready for dunking in warm au jus broth.

INGREDIENTS

3½ pounds beef chuck roast

1½ teaspoons salt

1 teaspoon freshly ground black pepper

½ teaspoon dried oregano

½ teaspoon dried thyme

1 tablespoon olive oil

1 (1.9-ounce) packet dry onion soup mix (see note, below)

3 cloves garlic, minced

2⅓ cups low-sodium beef broth

1 cup cola (not diet)

2 tablespoons low-sodium soy sauce

1 tablespoon Worcestershire sauce

FOR SERVING

8 hoagie or sub rolls

2 tablespoons unsalted butter

16 slices Swiss or provolone cheese

INSTRUCTIONS

1. Season all sides of roast with salt, pepper, oregano, and thyme.

2. Heat oil in a large nonstick skillet over medium-high heat. Once hot, add meat to the pan and sear, rotating slowly, until browned on all sides.

3. Place meat in a slow cooker and sprinkle with onion soup mix and garlic. Pour broth, cola, soy sauce, and Worcestershire sauce on top.

4. Cook on low for 4 hours, then remove meat to a cutting board. Thinly slice the meat, return it to the slow cooker, and continue to cook on low for 1 more hour.

5. When ready to serve, preheat the broiler. Slice rolls in half and lightly butter the top halves. Add a few slices of meat to the bottom half of each roll and top with two slices of cheese.

6. Broil for a few minutes, just until the cheese is melted and the bread is golden. Ladle the au jus broth from the slow cooker into small bowls for dipping.

VARIATIONS

PHILLY STYLE: Add caramelized onions, bell peppers, and mushrooms.

FOR SOME HEAT: Add jalapeños, yellow pepper rings, or crushed red pepper flakes.

LAUREN'S TIPS
DRY ONION SOUP MIX

You can use a store-bought onion soup packet for this recipe, or make your own. Visit tastesbetterfromscratch.com/homemade-dry-onion-soup-mix for my homemade recipe!

Pad Thai

I wanted to create an approachable pad Thai recipe that anyone could make in their home kitchen, and the result is just fantastic! It's so fresh and flavorful and is on the table in under thirty minutes.

INGREDIENTS

8 ounces flat rice noodles

3 tablespoons olive oil, divided

8 ounces uncooked shrimp, chicken, or extra-firm tofu, cut into small pieces

1 red bell pepper, thinly sliced

3 cloves garlic, minced

2 eggs

1 cup fresh bean sprouts

½ cup dry-roasted peanuts

3 green onions, chopped

½ cup chopped cilantro

2 limes

SAUCE

¼ cup + 1 tablespoon packed light brown sugar

3 tablespoons fish sauce

2 tablespoons rice vinegar (see note, below)

2 tablespoons creamy peanut butter (optional)

1 tablespoon low-sodium soy sauce

1 tablespoon Sriracha hot sauce, or more to taste

INSTRUCTIONS

1. Cook noodles according to package instructions just until tender. Rinse under cold water and set aside.

2. Mix all sauce ingredients together. Set aside.

3. Heat 1½ tablespoons oil in a large saucepan or wok over medium-high heat. Add shrimp, chicken, or tofu, bell pepper, and garlic. For shrimp, cook quickly, 1 to 2 minutes on each side, or until pink. If using chicken, cook until just cooked through, 3 to 4 minutes, flipping only once. Cook tofu until warmed through.

4. Push everything to the side of the pan. Add remaining 1½ tablespoons oil and the beaten eggs. Cook, scrambling into small pieces until egg is cooked. Add noodles, sauce, bean sprouts, and peanuts, reserving some peanuts for topping at the end. Toss everything to combine.

5. Top with green onions, extra peanuts, cilantro, and lime wedges. Serve immediately.

LAUREN'S TIPS

RICE VINEGAR

A more authentic substitution is 2 tablespoons tamarind paste, if you have access to it.

Cajun Chicken Pasta

I can have this pasta dish ready in thirty minutes and it hits the spot every single time! I love the creamy Cajun flavors in the sauce, and I like to throw in whatever fresh veggies I have in the fridge that need to be used.

INGREDIENTS

8 ounces farfalle pasta

2 tablespoons unsalted butter

3 cloves garlic, minced

1 pound boneless, skinless chicken breasts (about 2 breasts), cut into bite-size pieces

Fresh vegetables, such as 1 bell pepper, chopped, or 1 cup chopped broccoli florets, chopped asparagus, sliced zucchini, sliced mushrooms, or spinach (optional)

2 teaspoons Cajun seasoning, or more or less to taste

1 cup milk

4 ounces softened cream cheese, cut into small pieces

¾ cup freshly grated Parmesan cheese

½ teaspoon salt, or more to taste

½ teaspoon freshly ground black pepper

INSTRUCTIONS

1. Cook pasta according to package instructions until al dente. Drain, rinse with cold water, and set aside.

2. In a large pot or skillet, melt butter over medium heat. Add garlic and stir for 30 seconds.

3. Add chicken and vegetables, if using, and season with Cajun seasoning. Cook for 3 to 4 minutes, until chicken is nearly cooked through.

4. Add milk and cream cheese, stirring well until cream cheese has melted and sauce is smooth, 2 to 3 minutes.

5. Stir in pasta, Parmesan cheese, salt, and pepper. Serve immediately.

LAUREN'S TIPS

HEALTHIER SWAPS

Use whole-grain pasta, substitute olive oil for the butter, and use low-fat cream cheese and skim milk.

Beef Stroganoff

Delicious homemade Beef Stroganoff is a quick thirty-minute meal, with seared juicy beef strips smothered in sour cream mushroom gravy.

INGREDIENTS

1 pound egg noodles

1½ pounds boneless ribeye
   (see note, below)

1¼ teaspoons salt

¾ teaspoon freshly ground black
   pepper

1 tablespoon vegetable or canola oil

3 tablespoons unsalted butter

1 onion, chopped

8 ounces white button or cremini
   mushrooms, cut into thick slices

1½ tablespoons cornstarch

3 cups beef broth

1 tablespoon Worcestershire sauce

¾ cup sour cream

2 teaspoons Dijon mustard

Chopped fresh parsley or chives,
   for garnish (optional)

LAUREN'S TIPS

BEEF

For best results, use high-quality, quick-cooking steak that is marbled with fat, like beef sirloin, boneless ribeye, or beef tenderloin steak. For an inexpensive version, substitute ground beef, crumbling into pieces and cooking all the way through.

FUN TWIST

Try this dish served over mashed potatoes instead of egg noodles.

INSTRUCTIONS

1. Cook egg noodles according to package instructions. Drain and set aside.

2. Meanwhile, slice beef into thin slices against the grain. Cut long pieces in half, and discard any excess fat. Season with salt and pepper.

3. Heat a large skillet over high heat. Add oil and swirl to coat the bottom of the pan. Once hot, working in two batches, cook steak in a single layer for about 30 seconds, untouched, then flip to the other side and cook for 30 seconds to sear on all sides. Remove to a plate.

4. Reduce heat to medium-high and add butter to the pan. Add onions and mushrooms and cook for 5 to 8 minutes, stirring only occasionally, until tender.

5. Place cornstarch in a small bowl and whisk in a little beef broth until cornstarch dissolves. Add to the pan with remaining beef broth and Worcestershire sauce. Bring to a simmer and cook until slightly thickened.

6. Remove from the heat and stir in sour cream and Dijon. Taste and season with additional salt and pepper as needed.

7. Return beef to the pot, including juices from the plate. Cook for 1 minute.

8. Serve over hot cooked egg noodles. Garnish with fresh chopped parsley or chives, if using.

Homemade Spaghetti Sauce

A pot of delicious homemade spaghetti sauce simmering on the stove will have everyone excited for dinner. And you probably already have what you need to make it.

INGREDIENTS

1 pound ground beef (or half ground beef, half ground pork sausage)

½ teaspoon salt

¼ teaspoon freshly ground black pepper

1 medium onion, chopped

1 (15-ounce) can tomato sauce

1 (6-ounce) can tomato paste

1 tablespoon Worcestershire sauce

1 tablespoon granulated sugar

1 tablespoon dried parsley flakes

1 teaspoon garlic powder

½ teaspoon Italian seasoning

Crushed red pepper flakes, to taste

1 cup water

¼ cup fresh basil leaves (optional)

12 ounces cooked spaghetti, for serving

INSTRUCTIONS

1. Season ground beef with salt and pepper and cook in a large skillet over medium heat, crumbling into pieces, until browned. Remove grease. Add chopped onion and cook for 2 minutes.

2. Add tomato sauce, tomato paste, Worcestershire sauce, sugar, parsley, garlic powder, Italian seasoning, and crushed red pepper, to taste. Stir well to combine and bring to a low boil. Stir in water, reduce heat, and simmer for 30 minutes.

3. Add chopped basil, if using, before serving over spaghetti.

HOW TO FREEZE

Transfer to a freezer bag or freezer-safe container and freeze for up to 3 months. Rewarm on the stove.

Prep Time	Cook Time	Total Time	Yield
5 MINUTES	35 MINUTES	40 MINUTES	SERVES 6

Baked Ziti

This warm, cheesy pasta is the ultimate one-pan wonder, especially when we're craving an easy, comforting pasta dish on a busy night.

INGREDIENTS

1 teaspoon olive oil

½ pound ground hot Italian sausage

5 to 6 cloves garlic, minced

¼ teaspoon crushed red pepper flakes

1 (14½-ounce) can diced tomatoes

1 (8-ounce) can tomato sauce

1 tablespoon dried basil

½ teaspoon dried oregano

3 cups water

12 ounces ziti or penne pasta

½ cup half-and-half or heavy cream

½ cup freshly grated Parmesan cheese

Salt and freshly ground black pepper, to taste

1 cup shredded mozzarella cheese

INSTRUCTIONS

1. Heat olive oil in a deep, 12-inch or larger oven-safe skillet over medium heat. Add sausage and cook, crumbling into small pieces, until browned.

2. Add garlic and crushed red pepper flakes and cook for 1 minute. Stir in diced tomatoes, tomato sauce, basil, and oregano. Reduce heat and simmer, stirring occasionally, for 5 to 10 minutes.

3. Add water and uncooked pasta. Bring to a boil, cover, reduce heat to a low boil and cook, stirring occasionally, for 10 to 15 minutes, or until pasta is tender.

4. Stir in half-and-half and Parmesan cheese and season with salt and pepper to taste. Sprinkle mozzarella evenly on top.

5. Turn the broiler to high. Transfer the skillet to the oven and cook until the cheese is bubbly.

HOW TO FREEZE

Prepare the recipe, but don't bake. Cover tightly with aluminum foil sprayed lightly with nonstick cooking spray. Freeze for up to 3 months. Thaw overnight in the refrigerator, then bake for an additional 15 to 20 minutes. Or bake from frozen, covered in foil, for 1 hour and 15 minutes, then uncover and bake 20 to 30 minutes longer, or until warmed through.

Spaghetti Pie

This baked spaghetti pie recipe is easy enough for a busy weeknight meal and sure to be loved by the entire family. It makes a great take-and-bake meal for a family or friend in need.

INGREDIENTS

8 ounces spaghetti

3 tablespoons unsalted butter

1 large egg, beaten

1 cup freshly grated Parmesan cheese

¼ cup chopped fresh basil leaves

Salt and freshly ground black pepper, to taste

1 cup cottage cheese or ricotta

1½ cups homemade spaghetti sauce (page 95), or 1 (12-ounce) jar

INSTRUCTIONS

1. Preheat the oven to 350°F. Lightly grease a 9- or 10-inch deep-dish pie pan with cooking spray (see note, below).

2. Cook spaghetti according to package directions. Drain and transfer hot noodles to a large bowl.

3. Add butter and toss until butter melts. Add beaten egg, Parmesan cheese, basil, and a little salt and pepper and toss to combine. Pour into the prepared pie dish and pat firmly into the pan.

4. Spread cottage cheese evenly over the top. Spoon spaghetti sauce on top and smooth into an even layer.

5. Bake for 20 minutes. Allow to cool for 5 to 10 minutes before slicing into wedges and serving.

MAKE AHEAD

This pie can be made up to 2 days ahead. Assemble the pie in the dish, cover, and refrigerate until ready to bake.

- - - - - - - - -

HOW TO FREEZE

Assemble the pie in a freezer-safe baking dish. Cover with a double layer of aluminum foil (spray the bottom layer of foil with nonstick cooking spray) and freeze for up to 3 months. Bake from frozen, covered, for about 1 hour 15 minutes. Then uncover and bake until heated through, 20 to 30 minutes.

LAUREN'S TIPS

PIE PAN

If you don't have a deep-dish pie pan, use an 8-x-8-inch or similar size baking dish.

Classic Italian Lasagna

Unlike other lasagna recipes, we ditch the ricotta here in favor of a simple bechamel white sauce, and pair it with homemade red sauce to make the best lasagna ever. I always double this recipe and freeze the extra pan for another day. Buon appetito!

LASAGNA

9 regular lasagna noodles

1 pound shredded mozzarella cheese

8 ounces freshly grated Parmesan cheese

10 fresh basil leaves, chopped

RED SAUCE (or see Quicker Tip, right)

½ pound ground beef

½ pound ground Italian sausage

1 tablespoon olive oil

4 cloves garlic, minced

½ large onion, chopped

1½ cups fresh spinach leaves

½ bell pepper, chopped

1 (15-ounce) can tomato sauce

1 (6-ounce) can tomato paste

1 (14½-ounce) can diced tomatoes

2 teaspoons Italian seasoning

Salt and freshly ground black pepper, to taste

BÉCHAMEL (White Sauce)

4 tablespoons (½ stick) unsalted butter

¼ cup all-purpose flour

2½ cups milk

Salt and freshly ground black pepper, to taste

RED SAUCE

1. In a large skillet, brown the ground beef and sausage over medium-high heat, breaking the meat into pieces with a wooden spoon. When cooked through, remove the grease. Transfer meat to a food processor and pulse just 3 to 4 times, until it's broken up into very small pieces. Transfer to a bowl and set aside.

2. Add oil to the skillet over medium heat. Once hot, add onion, spinach, and bell pepper and cook until softened, 2 to 3 minutes. Add garlic and cook for a few seconds. Add veggies to the food processor and pulse several times until nearly pureed.

3. Return veggies to the skillet, add tomato sauce and tomato paste, and stir to combine. Add diced tomatoes, Italian seasoning, salt and pepper, and cooked ground beef. Stir well, cover, and simmer on low heat for 20 to 30 minutes, stirring occasionally.

4. While the red sauce simmers, boil the lasagna noodles for half the time suggested on the box. Drain into a large colander and rinse with water.

BÉCHAMEL

1. Heat the butter in a medium saucepan over medium heat. Once melted, add the flour and cook, stirring constantly, for 2 minutes.

2. Gradually add the milk, whisking until smooth. Season with salt and pepper.

3. Cook over medium heat, whisking often, until thickened, 5 to 7 minutes.

ASSEMBLY

1. Preheat the oven to 350°F. Lightly grease a deep 9-x-13-inch baking dish with cooking spray.

2. Arrange three noodles to line the bottom of the pan. Spread one-third of the red sauce over the noodles and sprinkle fresh basil on top. Spoon one-third of the white sauce into an even layer, followed by one-third of the Parmesan and mozzarella cheeses. Repeat layers two more times.

You may substitute 48 ounces bottled pasta sauce instead of making the red sauce from scratch. Heat in a saucepan and add cooked meat to it.

- - - - - - - - -

MAKE AHEAD

The entire lasagna can be assembled up to 2 days ahead of time and stored in the refrigerator. Remove from the fridge to come to room temperature, then bake as instructed. The red sauce and white sauce can also be made 1 to 2 days in advance and stored separately in the fridge.

- - - - - - - - -

HOW TO FREEZE

To freeze unbaked lasagna, cover well with a double layer of aluminum foil and freeze for up to 2 months. Thaw completely in the refrigerator, then bake covered for 30 minutes, then uncovered for 15 to 20 minutes more, or until cheese is bubbly. Or, bake from frozen, covered, for 1½ hours, then uncover and bake for another 35 to 45 minutes.

3. Bake for 30 minutes, or until the cheese is bubbly and golden. Rest for 30 minutes before slicing and serving.

Grilled Fish Tacos

This recipe has ruined restaurant fish tacos for me because I know I can make the best ones at home. These are so flavorful and garnished with all the best toppings, including shredded cabbage, pico de gallo, and a simple homemade crema.

INGREDIENTS

- 1 pound lean white fish fillets (such as tilapia, halibut, mahi mahi, snapper, or cod)
- ¾ teaspoon salt
- ¼ teaspoon freshly ground black pepper
- 2 tablespoons vegetable or canola oil
- Juice of 1 small lime
- 1 clove garlic, minced
- 1½ teaspoons chili powder
- 1 teaspoon ground cumin
- ½ teaspoon paprika
- ¼ teaspoon cayenne (optional)
- 8 white corn tortillas

CREMA SAUCE

- ½ cup sour cream
- ⅓ cup mayonnaise
- Juice of 1 small lime
- 1 teaspoon sriracha hot sauce, or to taste
- ½ teaspoon garlic powder
- ½ teaspoon cumin
- ¼ teaspoon salt

TOPPINGS

Pico de gallo

Cotija cheese

Shredded cabbage

Chopped cilantro

Sliced avocado

Lime wedges

Thinly sliced red onion

Hot sauce

INSTRUCTIONS

1. Season fish with salt and pepper on both sides.

2. In a mixing bowl, whisk together oil, lime juice, garlic, chili powder, cumin, paprika, and cayenne, if using. Place fish in a large resealable bag and pour the marinade on top. Refrigerate for 20 to 30 minutes.

3. Preheat a grill to medium-high heat. Brush grill grates with oil and grill fish fillets for 3 to 4 minutes on each side (cook time will vary depending on thickness of fish), flipping only once.

4. Meanwhile, combine all ingredients for the crema sauce in a small bowl and stir to mix. Set aside.

5. Transfer fish to a plate and allow to rest for a few minutes before gently breaking into pieces.

6. Add corn tortillas to the grill and warm for about 15 seconds on each side.

7. Serve fish on warm tortillas, topped with the crema sauce and your desired toppings. Serve with a side of Authentic Mexican Rice (page 176).

Street Tacos

My family goes crazy for these grilled chicken tacos, and I love how easy they are to make. Marinated chicken thighs are grilled to perfection and served with warmed corn tortillas, pico de gallo, and cilantro.

MARINATED CHICKEN

¼ cup orange juice

2 tablespoons apple cider vinegar

1½ tablespoons lime juice

3 cloves garlic, minced

1½ tablespoons chipotle chili powder

2 teaspoons dried oregano

2 teaspoons paprika

1 teaspoon salt

½ teaspoon freshly ground black pepper

¼ teaspoon ground cinnamon

1½ pounds boneless, skinless chicken thighs

TACOS

24 mini white corn tortillas (or 12 regular size)

2 cups pico de gallo

½ cup chopped fresh cilantro

Hot sauce (optional; our favorite for Mexican food is Valentina)

Sour cream (optional)

Fresh lime juice

INSTRUCTIONS

1. For the marinated chicken, combine all ingredients except the chicken in a bowl or resealable bag. Add chicken and refrigerate for 1 to 6 hours.

2. Preheat a grill to medium-high and grease the grates with oil.

3. Remove chicken from marinade and place on the hot grill. Cook for 4 to 5 minutes on each side, flipping once, until the thickest part registers about 165°F. Transfer to a plate and allow to rest for 10 minutes before chopping into small pieces.

4. Warm tortillas quickly on grill. To serve, layer two warmed mini corn tortillas together. Top with chopped chicken, pico de gallo, cilantro, and hot sauce and sour cream, if using. Spritz with fresh lime juice. Serve immediately.

HOW TO FREEZE

Place marinade and chicken in a freezer bag and freeze for up to 3 months. Thaw in the refrigerator before cooking. Cooked chicken may also be frozen for 3 months.

One-Pan Fajitas

This may be my favorite one-pan meal because it's dang delicious, includes lots of veggies, and I can make it ahead of time so that dinner time is a breeze.

INGREDIENTS

1½ pounds boneless, skinless chicken breasts

3 bell peppers (green, yellow, and red), thinly sliced

1 yellow onion, thinly sliced

2 cloves garlic, minced

3 tablespoons vegetable or canola oil

1 lime

¼ cup chopped fresh cilantro

12 small flour tortillas

Sour cream, shredded cheese, Guacamole (page 168), and Salsa (page 171) for topping (optional)

FAJITA SEASONING

1 tablespoon chili powder

1½ teaspoons paprika

1½ teaspoons cumin

½ teaspoon onion powder

½ teaspoon garlic powder

¼ teaspoon dried oregano

¼ teaspoon cayenne pepper (optional)

Salt and freshly ground black pepper

INSTRUCTIONS

1. Preheat the oven to 425°F. Lightly grease a large sheet pan with nonstick cooking spray.

2. Cut chicken against the grain into ½-inch strips. Place chicken on one half of the prepared pan and peppers and onions on the other.

3. Combine all seasoning ingredients together in a small bowl. Sprinkle most of the seasoning over the chicken, and some over the vegetables. Spoon minced garlic on top of the chicken and drizzle olive oil over the entire pan. Toss everything well and spread it into an even layer.

4. Cook for 15 to 20 minutes, or until chicken is cooked through. Wrap flour tortillas in foil and place them in the oven to warm during the last 5 minutes of cooking.

5. Remove everything from the oven. Squeeze fresh lime juice over chicken and vegetables and sprinkle with cilantro. Serve in warm tortillas with toppings, if desired.

HOW TO FREEZE

Prepare as instructed through step 3, then transfer to a freezer bag. Freeze for 2 to 3 months. Thaw in the fridge before cooking as instructed.

MAKE AHEAD

Cut and season the vegetables and chicken up to 1 day in advance and store in the fridge.

Baked Tacos

Don't expect leftovers with these amazing crunchy, baked meat-and-bean tacos. Everyone loves them, and I love how quick and easy they are to make.

INGREDIENTS

1 pound lean ground beef or ground turkey

1 small onion, chopped

1 tablespoon chili powder

1½ teaspoons ground cumin

½ teaspoon paprika

¼ teaspoon dried oregano

¼ teaspoon garlic powder

¾ teaspoon salt

½ teaspoon freshly ground black pepper

1 (16-ounce) can pinto beans or black beans, rinsed and drained

1 (8-ounce) can tomato sauce

20 hard tacos shells

1½ cups shredded cheddar cheese

1 romaine heart, finely chopped

2 Roma tomatoes, chopped

Salsa (page 171 or store-bought) and sour cream, for topping (optional)

INSTRUCTIONS

1. Cook ground beef in a large skillet over medium heat, crumbling it into small pieces, until browned. Remove grease and return to the heat. Add onion and cook for 3 minutes. Stir in all the spices.

2. Add beans and tomato sauce and stir to combine. Reduce the heat to low and simmer for 5 to 10 minutes, stirring occasionally.

3. Preheat the oven to 375°F. Divide hard taco shells among two 9-x-13-inch pans. Spoon taco mixture inside, and top with cheese. Bake for 10 to 15 minutes.

4. Serve topped with lettuce, tomato, sour cream, and salsa, if using.

HOW TO FREEZE

Transfer meat filling to a freezer bag and freeze for up to 3 months. Thaw overnight in the refrigerator, then fill tacos and bake as directed.

MAKE AHEAD

The meat filling can be made and refrigerated 2 to 3 days in advance, depending on the freshness of your ingredients.

Crispy Southwest Wraps

I threw together this recipe one night in an effort to use up some leftovers and canned pantry items and transform them into something my kids would eat. Little did I know it would turn into one of their favorite meals, and we now make them often.

INGREDIENTS

1 pound lean ground beef

½ teaspoon salt

¼ teaspoon freshly ground black pepper

2½ teaspoons chili powder

1½ teaspoons cumin

½ teaspoon garlic powder

2 tablespoons water

1 (15-ounce) can black beans, drained and rinsed

1 cup frozen corn, thawed

½ bell pepper, chopped

1 or 2 green onions, chopped

1 cup cooked rice (any kind of leftover rice works great)

1½ cups freshly shredded cheddar, Monterey Jack, mozzarella, or pepper jack cheese

8 large flour tortillas

½ cup sour cream

Salsa (page 171 or store-bought), for serving

INSTRUCTIONS

1. Heat ground beef in a large skillet over medium heat and cook, crumbling into small pieces, until browned. Remove grease.

2. Season with a little salt and pepper and add chili powder, cumin, garlic powder, and water. Stir to combine. Add black beans, corn, bell pepper, and green onions. Sauté for 2 to 3 minutes.

3. Heat another large skillet over medium-high heat. Warm the rice.

4. Spread a handful of cheese evenly spread across each tortilla, then add a small scoop of rice, placing it in a line along one end of the tortilla.

5. Top the rice with a few small dollops of sour cream and a spoonful of the beef filling. Starting at that end, roll the tortilla up, folding in the sides like a burrito. Repeat with the remaining tortillas and filling.

6. Spray the skillet generously with cooking spray and, working in batches if needed, place the wraps seam-side down on the greased skillet.

7. Brush the outside of each wrap with oil or spray them with cooking spray. Turn the wraps every minute or two until they are golden and crispy on all sides.

8. Serve warm, with salsa for dipping.

MAKE AHEAD

The meat filling can be made 2 to 3 days in advance and stored in the refrigerator.

HOW TO FREEZE

Assemble wraps up through step 5, then place in a freezer bag and freeze for up to 3 months. Thaw overnight in the fridge, then cook in a skillet until warmed through and crispy.

Navajo Tacos

It's the delicious Indian fry bread that makes a Navajo taco truly great. And with only four ingredients needed for the dough, it can't get any easier to make yourself. Serve with a big scoop of chili or your favorite kind of taco meat and all the toppings you like.

INDIAN FRY BREAD

2 cups all-purpose flour

2½ teaspoons baking powder

1 teaspoon salt

1 cup hot water

3 cups vegetable oil, for frying

TOPPINGS

2½ cups Classic Homemage Chili (page 148), taco-seasoned ground beef, or seasoned shredded pork, chicken, or beef

2 cups finely chopped lettuce

1 cup shredded cheese

1 cup chopped tomatoes

1 avocado, or Guacamole (page 168)

½ cup sliced olives

½ cup sour cream

½ cup Salsa (page 171 or store-bought)

MAKE AHEAD

The fry bread dough can be made up to 1 day ahead of time and stored in the fridge. Allow to come to room temperature before rolling out.

INSTRUCTIONS

1. In a large bowl, combine flour, baking powder, and salt. Add hot water and mix with a spoon until a dough forms (it will be sticky). Mix and knead the dough for 2 to 3 minutes.

2. Grease a clean bowl with a little oil or nonstick cooking spray. Add dough and turn once to coat it in oil. Cover bowl and allow to rest at room temperature for 1 to 2 hours.

3. Preheat the oven to 200°F.

4. Divide dough into six equal pieces. Roll and pat each piece into a flat disc, about ¼ inch thick. Cover dough discs with plastic wrap as you go to keep them from drying out.

5. Pour about 2 inches of oil into a pot or frying pan and heat over medium heat for 5 to 10 minutes, until oil reaches around 355°F.

6. If desired, cut a small slit in the center of each dough disc—this will help the fry bread cook flat, instead of forming a bowl shape. Working in batches, fry each disc in the hot oil until the dough is golden brown on one side, then carefully flip with tongs and fry on the other side. Set on a paper towel to drain, then place in the oven to keep hot while the remaining fry bread cooks.

7. **TO SERVE:** Top each piece of fry bread with a scoop of warm chili or meat. Pile high with your favorite toppings, like lettuce, shredded cheese, tomatoes, olives, sour cream, and guacamole.

VARIATION

DESSERT FRY BREAD: Serve warm fry bread topped with powdered sugar and honey, or cinnamon sugar.

Green Chile Chicken Enchiladas

When I think of classic Tex-Mex, these delicious enchiladas always come to mind. They require only basic pantry ingredients, and their mild spice and rich flavor make them popular with kids and adults alike.

INGREDIENTS

2 cups cooked, shredded chicken

2 cups shredded mozzarella cheese, divided

½ teaspoon ground cumin

½ teaspoon dried oregano

½ teaspoon freshly ground black pepper

8 (8-inch) flour tortillas or 16 (4-inch) corn tortillas

SAUCE

4 tablespoons (½ stick) unsalted butter

¼ cup flour

2 cups chicken broth

½ teaspoon ground cumin

½ teaspoon garlic powder

½ teaspoon dried oregano

¾ cup sour cream or plain Greek yogurt

8 ounces diced green chiles

FOR SERVING

Pico de gallo or Salsa (page 171 or store-bought)

Guacamole (page 168) or sliced avocado

Authentic Mexican Rice (page 176)

INSTRUCTIONS

1. Preheat the oven to 375°F. Grease a 9-x-13-inch baking dish.

2. Combine chicken, 1¼ cups shredded cheese, cumin, oregano, and black pepper in a bowl and stir to combine.

3. Fill each tortilla with a handful of the chicken mixture, roll tightly, and place seam-side down in the prepared baking dish.

4. Melt butter in a medium saucepan over medium heat. Whisk in flour and cook for 1 to 2 minutes. Whisk in broth, cumin, garlic powder, and oregano and cook, stirring often, until the mixture thickens, about 5 minutes. Remove from the heat and stir in sour cream and green chiles.

5. Pour the sauce over the enchiladas in the pan. Top with remaining ¾ cup shredded cheese and bake for 20 minutes.

6. Serve topped with fresh pico de gallo or salsa and guacamole or sliced avocado, with Mexican rice on the side.

MAKE AHEAD

The chicken filling and sauce can be made 1 to 2 days ahead of time and stored separately in the refrigerator.

Taco Pie

This easy Taco Pie is like a Tex-Mex twist on lasagna, with layers of meat-and-bean taco filling, corn tortillas, and shredded cheese. It's always a dinner winner!

INGREDIENTS

3 cups cooked chopped chicken

1 (10½-ounce) can condensed cream of chicken soup (see note, below)

1 (10-ounce) can diced tomatoes with green chilies

1 (15-ounce) can black beans, drained and rinsed

½ green bell pepper, diced

1 (1-ounce) packet taco seasoning

10 corn tortillas

1½ cups cheddar or Mexican blend cheese, divided

FOR TOPPING

Sour cream

Freshly chopped cilantro

Chopped avocado

INSTRUCTIONS

1. Preheat the oven to 350°F. Lightly grease a 9-inch pie dish.

2. In a large bowl, combine chicken, cream of chicken soup, diced tomatoes with green chilies, black beans, green bell pepper, and taco seasoning.

3. Tear 5 of the corn tortillas apart into a few pieces and use them to line the bottom of the pie dish. Spread half the chicken mixture over the tortillas. Top with half of the cheese.

4. Tear remaining 5 corn tortillas and place on top. Add remaining filling, then top with remaining cheese.

5. Bake for 30 minutes, or until cheese is bubbly and mixture is warmed through. Serve topped with sour cream, chopped cilantro, and avocado.

MAKE AHEAD

Assemble through step 4 up to 1 day ahead and store, covered, in the fridge.

- - - - - - - - -

HOW TO FREEZE

Assemble taco pie in a freezer-safe pie dish and cover tightly with a double layer of aluminum foil. Freeze for up to 3 months. Thaw overnight in the refrigerator, then bake as directed.

LAUREN'S TIPS

MEAT

Swap chicken for 1 pound cooked ground beef, if desired.

CANNED SOUP

For a homemade alternative, visit tastesbetterfromscratch.com/condensed-cream-anything-soup/.

Grilled Marinated Chicken

Yet another classic staple from my childhood; I've made and served this recipe a million times for everything from team dinners to Sundays with the family. It's my go-to chicken recipe and always gets rave reviews.

INGREDIENTS

12 ounces lemon-lime soda (not diet)

½ cup low-sodium soy sauce

½ cup vegetable or canola oil

1 teaspoon plain horseradish or horseradish sauce

1 teaspoon garlic powder

2 pounds boneless chicken breasts, tenders, or thighs

INSTRUCTIONS

1. Combine soda, soy sauce, oil, horseradish, and garlic powder in a large resealable bag. Add chicken and refrigerate for 1 to 3 hours.

2. Heat the grill to medium. Spray with cooking spray or rub the grill grates lightly with oil. Lay chicken on the grill and cook for 4 to 8 minutes. Then flip and cook on the other side for an additional 4 to 8 minutes, until cooked through (at least 165°F internal temperature at its thickest part).

3. Transfer to a plate and let rest for a few minutes before serving.

HOW TO
COOK IN THE OVEN

Bake in a shallow baking pan at 400°F until chicken reaches 165°F, 12 to 15 minutes for chicken tenders, 20 to 30 minutes for breasts, or 40 to 50 minutes for thighs.

- - - - - - - - -

HOW TO FREEZE

Place chicken and marinade in a freezer-safe resealable bag and lay flat in the freezer (it will be easier to store this way). Allow to thaw overnight in the fridge before cooking.

Teriyaki Chicken Stir-Fry

Get ready to fall in love with this delicious and easy teriyaki chicken recipe. With bite-size chicken pieces coated in homemade teriyaki sauce, it's ready to eat in less than thirty minutes.

INGREDIENTS

1 to 2 tablespoons olive oil

2 to 3 boneless, skinless chicken breasts, chopped

1 tablespoon cornstarch

1 tablespoon water

1 cup low-sodium soy sauce

¼ cup rice vinegar

2 tablespoons sesame oil

2 tablespoons honey

½ cup packed light brown sugar

2 cloves garlic, minced

1½ teaspoons ground ginger

¼ to ½ teaspoon crushed red pepper flakes

FOR SERVING

1 green onion, chopped

Hot cooked rice

Steamed broccoli or stir-fried veggies

INSTRUCTIONS

1. Heat oil in a skillet over medium-high heat. Add chicken and cook just until browned on both sides. Remove to a plate and cover to keep warm.

2. Stir cornstarch and water together to make a slurry. Add to the skillet along with all the remaining ingredients and stir well to combine. Lower the heat to medium and cook until it comes to a low boil. Boil for 1 minute. The sauce should be thick enough to coat the back of a spoon.

3. Stir in chicken and cook for a few more minutes, until chicken is cooked through.

4. Garnish with chopped green onion. Serve over cooked rice, with steamed vegetables on the side.

HOW TO FREEZE

Make the teriyaki sauce and allow it to cool. Combine sauce and raw chicken in a freezer bag and freeze for up to 3 months. Thaw overnight in the refrigerator, then pour into a pan and cook until chicken is cooked through.

MAKE AHEAD

Make the teriyaki sauce as described in step 2 and store in a container in the fridge for 3 to 5 days. When ready to eat, sauté the chicken, then pour sauce on top and cook until warmed through.

MAKE AHEAD

You can chop the veggies and make the rice and teriyaki sauce several hours or up to 1 day in advance; store them all separately in the fridge.

Grilled Hawaiian Chicken Teriyaki Bowls

These Hawaiian bowls may be the #1 reader favorite dinner recipe from tastesbetterfromscratch.com. With layers of coconut rice, grilled pineapple, chicken, and veggies topped with teriyaki sauce, it's no wonder they are so hugely popular.

COCONUT RICE

2 cups water

1½ cups canned unsweetened coconut milk (shake the can before using)

2 teaspoons packed light brown sugar

1 teaspoon salt

2 cups jasmine rice (about 13 ounces), well rinsed and drained

TERIYAKI SAUCE

2 teaspoons cornstarch

2 teaspoons water

½ cup low-sodium soy sauce

2 tablespoons rice vinegar

1 tablespoon sesame oil

1 tablespoon honey

¼ cup + 1 tablespoon packed light brown sugar

1 clove garlic, minced

¾ teaspoon ground ginger

¼ teaspoon crushed red pepper flakes

BOWLS

6 chicken tenders or 3 boneless chicken breasts

2 zucchini

2 bell peppers

1 red onion

½ pineapple, peeled and cut into spears

2 tablespoons olive oil

COCONUT RICE

1. Combine water, coconut milk, sugar, and salt in a large saucepan.

2. Bring to a boil, then stir in rice. Return to a boil. Reduce heat to low, cover, and cook for 20 minutes.

3. Remove from heat and let stand, covered, for 10 minutes before fluffing with a fork.

TERIYAKI SAUCE

1. Stir cornstarch and water together to make a slurry; place in a small saucepan.

2. Add all remaining teriyaki sauce ingredients and place over medium heat.

3. Bring to a boil, stirring constantly, and boil for about 1 minute. The sauce should be thick enough to coat the back of the spoon. Remove from the heat.

BOWLS

1. Pour ¼ cup teriyaki sauce over chicken and refrigerate to marinate for at least 15 minutes. Reserve remaining sauce.

2. Preheat the grill to medium-high and oil the grates.

3. If using a grill basket, chop vegetables into smaller chunks, otherwise chop them into pieces large enough that they will not fall through the grill grates.

4. Drizzle some olive oil over vegetables and pineapple spears. Grill vegetables and pineapple spears for 2 minutes on each side. Remove to a plate.

5. Remove chicken from marinade and place on hot grill. Cook for a few minutes on each side, flipping just once, until cooked through (at least 165°F internal temperature). Remove to a plate and let rest for 10 minutes before slicing.

6. Add a spoonful of coconut rice to each serving bowl. Top with grilled veggies, pineapple, and chicken. Drizzle some teriyaki sauce on top.

Butter Chicken

This is my take on one of my favorite Indian recipes, Butter Chicken. I love how the blend of spices and the creamy sauce come together in a rich and boldly flavorful chicken and gravy, served over rice.

MARINATED CHICKEN

½ cup plain yogurt

2 teaspoons minced fresh ginger

2 garlic cloves, minced

1¼ teaspoons salt

1 teaspoon ground turmeric

1 teaspoon garam masala

1 teaspoon ground cumin

¼ teaspoon freshly ground black pepper

1½ pounds boneless, skinless chicken breasts or thighs, cut into bite-size pieces

GRAVY

3 tablespoons unsalted butter or ghee, divided

1 cup finely chopped onion

1 small jalapeño, finely diced (seeds and ribs removed for less heat)

1 tablespoon grated fresh ginger

2 cloves garlic, minced

1 (14½-ounce) can petite diced tomatoes or 3 cups finely chopped tomatoes

¼ cup unsalted cashews (optional; see note, right)

1 tablespoon granulated sugar or honey

2 teaspoons garam masala

1 teaspoon ground cumin

1 teaspoon ground coriander

½ teaspoon chili powder

¼ to ½ teaspoon cayenne pepper

1¼ cups heavy cream or 1 (13½-ounce) can coconut milk

1 teaspoon dried crushed fenugreek leaves (optional)

INSTRUCTIONS

1. Combine all marinade ingredients in a bowl or resealable bag and stir to combine. Add chicken and refrigerate for 3 to 8 hours.

2. Heat 2 tablespoons butter in a large skillet over medium heat. Once melted, add onion and jalapeño and cook for 5 minutes, until translucent and soft. Add ginger and garlic and cook for 30 seconds. Add tomatoes and cashews and cook for 5 minutes.

3. Pour everything into a blender and blend until smooth. (If it's not smooth enough, you can pass it through a fine-mesh strainer.) Set aside.

4. Melt remaining 1 tablespoon butter in the skillet over medium-high heat. Add pureed mixture from the blender. Stir in sugar, garam masala, cumin, coriander, chili powder, and cayenne. Simmer for 20 minutes.

5. Meanwhile, cook chicken on the grill or in a cast iron skillet over medium-high heat until browned on both sides. Add to the pot with simmering sauce and continue cooking for 5 to 10 minutes, until chicken is cooked through. Stir in cream and crushed fenugreek leaves, if using. Taste and add additional seasonings or more cayenne for added heat, if desired.

6. Garnish with cilantro. Serve over cooked basmati rice with naan or chapati.

FOR SERVING

Hot cooked basmati rice

Naan or chapati

Cilantro, for garnish

LAUREN'S TIPS

CASHEWS

If you don't have a powerful blender, you can soak the cashews in water for 1 to 2 hours before adding them and they will blend more smoothly.

- - - - - - - - -

MAKE AHEAD

The sauce can be made and stored in the fridge 2 to 3 days in advance. I like to make the entire meal in the morning and keep it warm in my slow cooker until dinnertime. Leftovers also reheat well, if you want to make it a day or two in advance. I recommend using chicken thighs in this case, as they don't dry out as easily when reheated.

- - - - - - - - -

HOW TO FREEZE

Freeze for up to 3 months in an airtight container. Thaw overnight in the fridge before rewarming on the stove.

Panang Curry

Panang Curry might be my ultimate favorite kind of curry. It's bursting with rich and creamy flavor from the curry paste and coconut milk, and this hearty version is filled with chicken, veggies, and fresh basil.

INGREDIENTS

1 tablespoon canola oil

1 small onion, sliced

1 green bell pepper, thinly sliced

1 red bell pepper, thinly sliced

4 garlic cloves, minced

2 teaspoons freshly grated ginger

1 to 2 tablespoons Panang curry paste, depending on heat preference (see note, below)

1 tablespoon peanut butter

2 (14-ounce) cans coconut milk (Chaokoh brand is my favorite), divided

2 teaspoons cornstarch

2 pounds chicken breast, cut into pieces against the grain (or shrimp or tofu)

¼ cup packed light brown sugar

1 tablespoon fish sauce

1 tablespoon lime juice

1 cup loosely packed basil leaves, roughly chopped

Salt and freshly ground black pepper, to taste

5 cups cooked white, brown, or jasmine rice, for serving

INSTRUCTIONS

1. Heat oil over medium-high heat in a large nonstick skillet. Add onions and sauté for 2 minutes, then add bell peppers, garlic, and ginger and sauté for 2 minutes more.

2. Add curry paste and peanut butter and sauté for 1 minute. Add 1½ cans of coconut milk. Whisk cornstarch into remaining ½ can coconut milk, then add to the pan. Stir well.

3. Add chicken, stirring to coat. Simmer for 10 to 15 minutes, or just until chicken is no longer pink and sauce begins to thicken.

4. Stir in brown sugar, fish sauce, lime juice, and basil. Simmer for 5 minutes. Season with salt and pepper to taste.

5. Serve over hot cooked rice.

LAUREN'S TIPS

PANANG CURRY PASTE

I like the Mae Ploy Brand, which can be found on Amazon or at your local Asian market.

VEGGIES

This is a great recipe to clean out your veggie drawer. Try adding mushrooms, zucchini, bean sprouts, spinach, bamboo shoots, or carrots.

HOW TO FREEZE

Panang curry can be frozen in an airtight container for 2 to 3 months. Allow it to thaw overnight in the refrigerator and reheat on the stove or in the microwave. Cook rice fresh for serving.

One-Pan Jambalaya

When it comes to healthy, hearty comfort food, this chicken and sausage jambalaya can't be beat. I love the bold Cajun flavors and that it cooks in just one pan.

INGREDIENTS

1 tablespoon vegetable or canola oil

1 pound andouille sausage, sliced

½ pound boneless, skinless chicken breasts, cut into bite-size pieces

2 tablespoons unsalted butter

2 tablespoons all-purpose flour

1 small onion, chopped

3 ribs celery, chopped

1 medium bell pepper, chopped

3 to 4 green onions, chopped

2 cloves garlic, finely minced

1 (14½-ounce) can diced tomatoes

1 teaspoon dried basil

1 teaspoon Cajun seasoning

½ teaspoon granulated sugar

2 cups low-sodium chicken broth

1 cup long-grain white rice

INSTRUCTIONS

1. Heat oil in a large skillet with a fitted lid over medium-high heat. Add sausage and chicken and brown well, flipping once or twice to brown on all sides. (Chicken doesn't need to be cooked through.) Remove to a plate.

2. Add butter and flour to the pan and stir well, scraping up any leftover browned bits from the pan.

3. Add onion, celery, bell peppers, green onions, and garlic and sauté for a few minutes. Add tomatoes, basil, Cajun seasoning, and sugar and stir well to combine. Simmer for 2 minutes.

4. Add chicken broth, rice, and reserved meat. Bring mixture to a boil. Reduce the heat, cover pan with fitted lid, and cook for 20 to 25 minutes, or until water is absorbed.

5. Remove from the heat and allow to rest with the lid on for 10 minutes, then fluff with a fork and serve.

Prep Time	Cook Time	Total Time	Yield
10 MINUTES	25 MINUTES	35 MINUTES	SERVES 5

Sheet-Pan Sausage and Veggies

Yet another fantastic and healthy sheet-pan dinner that's ready in a cinch and packs so much flavor and heartiness. This is a great meal for any time of year, because you can swap in whatever produce is in season.

INGREDIENTS

12 to 16 ounces precooked sausage (see note, below), sliced into ½-inch-thick coins

2 cups diced potatoes (red, Yukon gold, or sweet potato)

2 cups fresh green beans, halved

1 head broccoli, cut into florets

1 bell pepper, chopped into 1-inch pieces

1 yellow squash, chopped into 1-inch pieces

⅓ cup olive oil

SEASONING

1 teaspoon garlic powder

1 teaspoon paprika

1 teaspoon Italian seasoning

1 teaspoon oregano

¾ teaspoon salt

½ teaspoon freshly ground black pepper

¼ teaspoon crushed red pepper flakes

GARNISH

Freshly grated Parmesan cheese (optional)

2 tablespoons chopped fresh parsley (optional)

Other veggies that work well:

- Yellow or red onion
- Trimmed asparagus
- Chopped carrots
- Zucchini
- Whole cherry tomatoes
- Brussels sprouts
- Cauliflower florets

INSTRUCTIONS

1. Preheat the oven to 400°F.

2. Combine sausage and all veggies in a large bowl and drizzle olive oil over the top. Add all the seasonings and toss everything to evenly coat.

3. Spread into an even layer on two sheet pans, or one extra-large (15-x-21-inch) sheet pan. Try to spread it out so nothing overlaps and all ingredients have the space to roast properly.

4. Bake for about 25 minutes, flipping/tossing everything on the pan once during cooking, until vegetables are tender.

5. Garnish with freshly grated Parmesan and chopped fresh parsley, if using.

LAUREN'S TIPS

FOR A HEARTIER MEAL

Serve with cooked quinoa, brown rice, warm tortillas, or Easy Artisan Bread (page 68).

SAUSAGES

We love Aidells Chicken and Apple Sausages or smoked sausages, but use your favorite kind.

- -

MAKE AHEAD

Prepare the sausage and veggies on the sheet pan(s) up to one day before cooking and store, covered, in the fridge.

Prep Time	Cook Time	Total Time	Yield
10 MINUTES	35 MINUTES	45 MINUTES	SERVES 6

Mini Meatloaves

I love cooking meatloaf in a muffin tin because it cooks faster and the mini meatloaves make for great portion control. We like to serve them with mashed potatoes and extra sauce on the side.

INGREDIENTS

1½ pounds lean ground beef or ground turkey

⅔ cup panko breadcrumbs

½ cup chopped onion

1 egg, lightly beaten

1 tablespoon barbecue sauce

1 tablespoon prepared yellow mustard

1½ teaspoons chili powder

½ teaspoon garlic powder

½ teaspoon salt

½ teaspoon freshly ground black pepper

SAUCE

½ cup ketchup

2 teaspoons Dijon mustard

⅓ cup packed light brown sugar

¼ teaspoon ground nutmeg

INSTRUCTIONS

1. Preheat the oven to 350°F. Grease a 12-cup muffin tin with nonstick cooking spray.

2. In a large mixing bowl, combine ground beef, breadcrumbs, onion, egg, barbecue sauce, mustard, chili powder, garlic powder, salt, and pepper and use your hands or a large spoon to mix.

3. Divide the mixture evenly among the 12 cups in the muffin tin, pressing down to fill each cup. Bake for 15 minutes.

4. In the meantime, in a small bowl mix together all the ingredients for the sauce.

5. Remove meatloaves from the oven and use a paper towel to soak up any grease on the tops.

6. Generously spoon sauce over each mini meatloaf and return to the oven for an additional 10 to 15 minutes, or until cooked through.

HOW TO FREEZE

Prepare the meatloaf and press it into a greased muffin tin. Cover well with plastic wrap and place the tray in the freezer to "flash freeze." After about 1 hour, remove the meatloaf muffins and place them in an air-tight container and freeze for up to 3 months. Thaw in the refrigerator before baking as instructed.

Marinated Flank Steak

Growing up, each child in my family got to choose their own birthday dinner. Most of us chose this flank steak recipe for our special meal, because it's just that good. It's a recipe that always reminds me of home.

INGREDIENTS

1 cup vegetable or canola oil

1 cup low-sodium soy sauce

1 cup peach juice or peach nectar

2 tablespoons dried minced onion

2 tablespoons dried parsley

1¾ pounds flank steak

INSTRUCTIONS

1. Combine oil, soy sauce, peach juice, minced onion, and parsley in a resealable bag or large bowl. Add flank steak and marinate in the fridge for 3 to 6 hours.

2. Remove from the fridge 20 minutes before grilling. Heat the grill to high heat.

3. Once the grill is hot, remove steak from the marinade and place on the grill.

4. Cook for 3 to 4 minutes, then flip to the other side and cook for 3 to 4 more minutes, depending on how well done you like your steak. Cook to an internal temperature of 125 to 130°F for rare, 140°F for medium-rare, or 150°F for medium.

5. Remove steak from the grill and place on a cutting board. Cover it with aluminum foil to keep warm, and allow it to rest for 5 to 10 minutes.

6. Cut the meat against the grain, at a diagonal, into very thin slices and serve.

Slow Cooker Ribs

The most crazy-tender pork ribs couldn't be easier to make thanks to this slow cooker method. The end result will knock your socks off!

INGREDIENTS

3 pounds pork ribs, baby back (recommended), spare, or country-style, cut into large sections

1½ teaspoons salt

1 teaspoon freshly ground black pepper

1 teaspoon garlic powder

1 teaspoon onion powder

1 teaspoon light brown sugar

32 ounces barbecue sauce

INSTRUCTIONS

1. Preheat the oven to 400°F. Remove membranes from the back of ribs, if needed.

2. Season ribs generously on both sides with salt and pepper. Rub garlic powder, onion powder, and brown sugar onto both sides of ribs.

3. Place ribs on a baking sheet and bake for 15 minutes. Flip ribs to the other side and bake for another 15 minutes.

4. Layer ribs in a 6-quart slow cooker. Pour barbecue sauce on top, reserving some sauce for serving.

5. Cover and cook on low for 4 to 6 hours. Brush ribs with extra barbecue sauce before serving.

Prep Time	Cook Time	Total Time	Yield
20 MINUTES	2 HOURS 40 MINUTES	3 HOURS	SERVES 4

Braised Short Ribs

If you're looking for an incredibly easy recipe with a huge wow factor, this is it! These ribs are restaurant quality and they couldn't be easier to make, cooked in just one pot.

INGREDIENTS

3 tablespoons olive oil, divided

1 yellow onion, diced

3 carrots, chopped

8 whole beef short ribs

1 teaspoon salt

¾ teaspoon freshly ground black pepper

¼ cup all-purpose flour

1 cup dry red wine (such as Côtes du Rhône or Pinot Noir)

2½ cups low-sodium beef broth

2 tablespoons tomato paste

2 sprigs fresh thyme

2 sprigs fresh rosemary

HOW TO FREEZE

Leftovers can be frozen for up to 3 months in an airtight container. Thaw overnight in the fridge and rewarm on the stove.

INSTRUCTIONS

1. Preheat the oven to 350°F.

2. In a large Dutch oven or oven-safe pot with a lid, heat 1 tablespoon of oil over medium-high heat. Add onion and carrots and cook for 5 minutes, stirring constantly. Remove veggies to a plate.

3. Season ribs with salt and pepper and coat on all sides with flour. Add remaining 2 tablespoons oil to the pot and turn heat to high. Add ribs and brown on all sides, about 45 seconds per side. Remove to a plate.

4. Add wine to deglaze the pan. Scrape the bottom of the pan to release any browned bits. Bring to a boil and cook 2 minutes.

5. Add beef broth, then stir in tomato paste. Add ribs, veggies, and whole sprigs of thyme and rosemary to the pot.

6. Cover with the lid and place in the oven. Cook for 2 hours, then reduce heat to 325°F and cook for an additional 30 to 45 minutes, until ribs are tender.

7. Remove the pot from the oven and allow to rest for 20 minutes with the lid on. Before serving, skim off any fat that has risen to the top.

8. Serve with mashed potatoes and a spoonful of gravy from the pot.

ALTERNATIVE COOKING METHODS

SLOW COOKER: Follow recipe through step 5, then transfer to a slow cooker to cook on low for 6 to 8 hours.

INSTANT POT: Prepare the recipe as instructed using your Instant Pot's sauté setting. Once everything is added to the pot, cook on manual/high pressure for 45 minutes. Allow pressure to naturally release before opening the lid and serving.

SOUP

Beef Stew

This flavorful, rich, and hearty beef stew includes tender beef, bacon, carrots, and potatoes in a delicious gravy broth. This recipe is restaurant quality, and you can make it on the stove, in the oven, or in a slow cooker or Instant Pot.

INGREDIENTS

8 ounces applewood-smoked bacon, chopped

2½ pounds chuck beef, cut into 1-inch cubes

1 teaspoon salt

¾ teaspoon freshly ground black pepper

⅓ cup + 3 tablespoons all-purpose flour, divided

Up to 2 tablespoons olive oil, as needed, divided

1 yellow onion, chopped

5 cloves garlic, minced

1 cup good quality dry red wine (such as Pinot Noir, Burgundy, or Côtes du Rhône)

2 tablespoons red wine vinegar

5 cups beef stock or broth

1 tablespoon tomato paste

2 teaspoons Better than Bouillon® beef base

2 bay leaves

1 teaspoon chopped fresh rosemary, or ½ teaspoon dried

1 teaspoon fresh thyme leaves, or ½ teaspoon dried

8 ounces white mushrooms, sliced (optional)

2 tablespoons unsalted butter (optional, if using mushrooms)

4 large carrots, peeled and sliced diagonally into chunks

½ pound mini gold or fingerling potatoes, cut into small chunks

8 ounces frozen whole pearl onions (optional)

Crushed red pepper flakes, to taste (optional)

Chopped fresh parsley, for garnish

INSTRUCTIONS

1. Heat chopped bacon in a large soup pot over medium-low heat. Cook, stirring occasionally, until crispy. Remove to a paper towel–lined plate. Reserve the pan with the bacon grease.

2. Pat beef cubes dry with paper towels and season all over with salt and pepper. Toss in ⅓ cup flour to coat on all sides.

3. Heat the pan with bacon grease over medium-high heat. Once hot, add the beef, cooking it in two to three batches so you don't overcrowd the pan, turning until all sides are browned. Add a little oil to the pot while searing, as needed. Remove meat to a plate and set aside.

4. Reduce heat to medium. Add chopped onion and cook for 2 to 3 minutes. Add garlic and cook for 30 seconds. Add wine and vinegar and increase the heat to medium-high, scraping up any browned bits from the bottom of the pan. Simmer for 10 minutes.

5. Add beef stock, tomato paste, beef base, bay leaves, rosemary, and thyme. Add beef and bacon back to the pot. Bring to a boil, then reduce heat to a simmer. Cover and cook for 1½ hours, or until beef is tender.

6. If using mushrooms, heat butter and 1 tablespoon olive oil in a sauté pan over medium-high heat. Add mushrooms to the pan in a single layer. Cook for several minutes without touching. Once golden on the bottom, flip to the other side and cook for a few more minutes.

7. Add mushrooms, carrots, potatoes, and pearl onions, if using, to the soup pot and cook for 15 to 20 more minutes, until carrots and potatoes are tender.

continued

continued from page 142

8. Taste broth. Season as needed with additional salt, pepper, bouillon, rosemary, thyme, or garlic powder. Add a sprinkle of crushed red pepper, if using.

9. Ladle some of the hot broth into a bowl and whisk the remaining 3 tablespoons flour into it until smooth. Add to pot and cook for 2 to 5 minutes, until broth has slightly thickened. Garnish with fresh parsley. Serve with Easy Artisan Bread (page 68).

ALTERNATE COOKING METHODS

OVEN BEEF STEW: Preheat the oven to 325°F and set a rack in the lower middle position. Prepare the recipe in an oven-safe pot up to adding the beef and bacon back in step 5. Cover and cook in the oven for 2½ to 3 hours, until meat is tender. During the last hour of cooking, dissolve the flour mixture in the broth and add it with potatoes, carrots, and mushrooms.

SLOW COOKER BEEF STEW: Cook bacon and brown meat and onions according to steps 1 through 5 above, then combine all ingredients listed in step 5 in a slow cooker. Cook on low for 6 to 8 hours, until tender. During the last 1½ hours of cooking, dissolve the flour mixture in the broth and add it with potatoes, carrots, and mushrooms.

INSTANT POT BEEF STEW: Brown bacon, meat, and onions using the sauté setting on your Instant Pot. Turn the Instant Pot off, add the remaining ingredients from step 5 above, and cook on high pressure for 35 minutes, with a 10-minute natural release. Add potatoes and carrots and cook on high pressure for 6 minutes. Stir in flour mixture at the end to thicken, and add mushrooms.

Corn Chowder

My favorite Corn Chowder recipe includes green chiles and chipotle peppers, which give it a unique, subtle spice and boost of flavor that I can't resist. It's always hugely popular.

INGREDIENTS

3 slices bacon, chopped

1 yellow onion, diced

2 ribs celery, chopped

2 tablespoons unsalted butter

4 cups corn, fresh or frozen (about 5 ears)

1 medium russet or gold potato, peeled and chopped

1 to 2 whole chipotle peppers in adobo sauce, finely diced (see note, below)

1 (4-ounce) can diced green chiles

½ teaspoon salt

4 cups low-sodium chicken broth

1½ cups half-and-half, cream, or whole milk

3 tablespoons cornmeal, plus more as needed

¼ cup water

INSTRUCTIONS

1. Cook bacon in a large soup pot over medium heat until crispy. Add onion and celery and cook, stirring, for 3 to 4 minutes.

2. Add butter and stir until melted. Add corn, potato, chipotle peppers, green chiles, and salt.

3. Slowly pour in chicken broth and half-and-half. Bring to a boil, then reduce the heat to low and simmer for 15 to 20 minutes.

4. Combine cornmeal with water and add to chowder. Cook for 5 more minutes, until soup has slightly thickened. It will continue to thicken as it cools, but if you want it thicker, add another tablespoon of cornmeal mixed with a little water.

LAUREN'S TIPS

CHIPOTLE PEPPERS IN ADOBO

Find them in a can in the Mexican food aisle at your local grocery store.

Broccoli Cheese Soup

This is my mom's delicious Broccoli Cheese Soup recipe, and I love how it's packed with fresh veggies and such wonderful flavor. We enjoy it with a salad and crusty bread.

INGREDIENTS

3 cups low sodium vegetable broth

1 cup grated carrot, (1 to 2 carrots)

1 cup finely diced celery,
(about 2 ribs celery)

1½ cups grated Yukon Gold or
russet potatoes (2 small/
medium potatoes)

4½ cups chopped broccoli
(about 3 small heads broccoli)

1 cup finely chopped yellow onion
(about 1 medium onion)

5 tablespoons unsalted butter,
divided

¼ cup all-purpose flour

2 cups half-and-half

1½ cups whole milk

Salt and freshly ground black
pepper, to taste

3 cups freshly grated cheddar
cheese, room temperature

INSTRUCTIONS

1. Heat vegetable broth in a large soup pot over medium heat. Add carrots, celery, and potatoes, cover, and bring to a boil. Once boiling, reduce the heat and simmer until vegetables are tender, 3 to 5 minutes.

2. Add chopped broccoli and cook at a simmer for 2 to 3 minutes. Remove from the heat.

3. In a separate skillet over medium heat, sauté onion in 1 tablespoon butter until tender and lightly browned. Add onion to the pot with vegetables.

4. Add remaining 4 tablespoons butter to the skillet over medium heat. Once melted, whisk in flour and stir well. Add half-and-half and milk 1 cup at a time, stirring constantly. Cook, stirring continually, until thickened. Season well with salt and pepper. Add to the pot of cooked vegetables, stirring carefully to combine.

5. Stir in grated cheese until melted. Taste and season with additional salt and pepper to taste, if needed.

ALTERNATIVE COOKING METHODS

INSTANT POT: Combine broth and all veggies in the Instant Pot. Cook on high pressure/manual for 2 minutes, then quick-release steam. Cook the butter and flour and the half-and-half and milk in a separate skillet as directed in step 4, and add to the Instant Pot. Stir in cheddar cheese.

SLOW COOKER: Combine broth and all vegetables in the slow cooker. Cook on high for 4 hours or low for 6 to 8 hours. Cook the butter and flour and the half-and-half and milk in a separate skillet as directed in step 4, and add to the slow cooker. Stir in cheddar cheese.

Classic Homemade Chili

Everyone needs a great no-frills, meat-and-bean chili recipe. This one is definitely worthy of your next chili cook-off.

INGREDIENTS

1 tablespoon olive oil

1 large onion, diced

2 pound lean ground beef

1 pound pork sausage

4 cups tomato juice (see note, below)

2 (15-ounce) cans pinto beans, undrained

1 (16-ounce) can kidney beans, undrained

1 (14½-ounce) can petite diced tomatoes, undrained

1 cup ketchup

¼ cup red wine vinegar

3 tablespoons chili powder

1 tablespoon packed brown sugar

1 teaspoon paprika

1 teaspoon ground cumin

¾ teaspoon garlic salt

½ teaspoon freshly ground black pepper

¼ teaspoon cayenne

Shredded cheddar cheese and Sour cream, for topping (optional)

INSTRUCTIONS

1. Heat olive oil in a large soup pot over medium-high heat. Once hot, add onion and cook for about 5 minutes, stirring occasionally.

2. Add ground beef and sausage and cook, breaking apart into small pieces with a wooden spoon, until browned. Remove grease.

3. Add tomato juice, pinto and kidney beans, diced tomatoes, ketchup, vinegar, chili powder, brown sugar, paprika, cumin, garlic salt, pepper, and cayenne.

4. Bring to a boil, stirring, then reduce the heat and simmer for 1 to 3 hours, stirring occasionally.

5. Taste and add additional seasoning, as needed, to taste. Serve in bowls with a dollop of sour cream and a sprinkle of cheese on top.

6. Serve chili with Buttermilk Cornbread (page 55), Buttermilk Biscuits (page 35), or a green salad.

VARIATIONS

MAKE IT SPICY: Add more cayenne pepper, chopped jalapeños (canned or fresh), or hot sauce.

SLOW COOKER: Cook the onion and brown the meat in a large skillet, then combine with all the remaining ingredients in a large slow cooker. Cook on low for 5 to 7 hours.

INSTANT POT: Cook the onion and brown the meat using the sauté setting, then drain the grease. Add everything else and cook on high pressure for 20 minutes. Allow pressure to naturally release.

HOW TO FREEZE

Freeze chili in a freezer-safe container for up to 3 months. Thaw overnight in the refrigerator, then reheat on the stovetop.

LAUREN'S TIPS
TOMATO JUICE

If you don't have tomato juice on hand, substitute 2 cups tomato sauce + 2 cups water.

Chicken Noodle Soup

This soup is easy to make on a weeknight if you have the broth on hand, and is made even better with a richly flavorful homemade broth (see Lauren's Tips). My kids get more excited for this soup than any other that I make.

SOUP

- ½ tablespoon unsalted butter
- 2 ribs celery, diced
- 3 to 4 large carrots, diced
- 1 clove garlic, minced
- 10 cups chicken broth
  (see note, below)
- 1 teaspoon salt, plus more to taste
- ½ teaspoon freshly ground black pepper, plus more to taste
- ⅛ teaspoon dried rosemary, plus more to taste
- ⅛ teaspoon dried sage
- ⅛ teaspoon crushed red pepper flakes
- 1 teaspoon Better than Bouillon® chicken base or chicken bouillon granules, or more as needed
- 5 cups dry egg noodles, farfalle, or other bite-size pasta
  (or homemade, see below)
- 3 cups chopped rotisserie chicken

INSTRUCTIONS

1. Heat butter, celery, and carrots in a large stock pot over medium-high heat. Sauté for 3 minutes. Add garlic and cook for another 30 seconds.

2. Add chicken broth and season with salt, pepper, rosemary, sage, and crushed red pepper. Taste and add a spoonful or more of chicken bouillon, as needed, to enhance the flavor.

3. Bring broth to a boil. Add noodles and cook until tender. If using store-bought noodles, be cautious not to overcook them! Keep in mind they will continue to cook once you remove the pot from the heat.

4. Add chicken. Taste again and add more seasonings, if needed.

LAUREN'S TIPS
BROTH

I highly recommend picking up a rotisserie chicken and using the meat in the soup, and the carcass to make simple homemade stock. Place the bones in a stockpot with 8 cups cold water. Chop 2 carrots, 2 onions, and 2 celery ribs and add to the pot, along with 1 teaspoon peppercorns and 2 bay leaves. Bring to a boil, then lower the heat and simmer for 2 hours. Or, cook in an Instant Pot on high pressure for 30 minutes.

CHICKEN

To use raw chicken meat, cook in the boiling broth just before adding the noodles.

HOMEMADE EGG NOODLES

Visit tastesbetterfromscratch.com/homemade-egg-noodles for my recipe. I love making them from scratch because you can't overcook them (they wont get soggy) and they only require four basic ingredients.

Chicken Tortilla Soup

I love how easy this recipe is easy to throw together and that it uses basic pantry ingredients. It's perfect for a comforting but healthy weeknight meal.

INGREDIENTS

1 tablespoon olive oil

1 bell pepper, diced

1 yellow onion, diced

4 cloves garlic, minced

1 (15-ounce) can black beans, drained and rinsed

1 (14½-ounce) can diced tomatoes

1 (4-ounce) can diced green chiles

1 cup fresh or frozen corn

5 cups low-sodium chicken broth

1 tablespoon chili powder

2 teaspoons ground cumin

1 teaspoon dried oregano

½ teaspoon paprika

Salt and freshly ground black pepper, to taste

2 to 3 boneless, skinless chicken breasts

1 tablespoon fresh lime juice

¼ cup chopped fresh cilantro

Shredded cheese, sour cream, avocado, tortilla chips, for topping (optional)

INSTRUCTIONS

1. Heat olive oil in a large pot over medium heat. Add bell pepper, onion, and garlic and sauté for 2 to 3 minutes, until the onion starts to soften.

2. Add black beans, diced tomatoes, green chiles, corn, chicken broth, chili powder, cumin, oregano, and paprika, and season with salt and pepper to taste. Bring soup to a simmer and cook for 15 to 20 minutes.

3. Cut chicken into a few pieces and add to the pot. Cook for 7 to 10 more minutes, until the chicken is cooked through.

4. Remove chicken and shred with forks, then return to the pot and add lime juice and cilantro.

5. Serve with desired toppings, like shredded cheese, sour cream, or avocado.

ALTERNATIVE COOKING METHODS

SLOW COOKER: After sautéing the vegetables in step 1, transfer them to a slow cooker along with the chicken broth, diced tomatoes, black beans, corn, chiles, spices, and chicken breasts. Cook on low for 4 to 6 hours or high for 2 to 3 hours. Remove chicken and shred with forks. Return to the soup and add lime juice and cilantro.

INSTANT POT: Cook vegetables and garlic on the sauté setting, then turn the pot off. Add chicken broth, diced tomatoes, black beans, corn, chiles, spices, and chicken. Cook on high pressure for 7 minutes with a 10-minute natural release. Shred chicken, then return it to the soup and add lime juice and cilantro.

Creamy Tomato Basil Soup

This Creamy Tomato Basil Soup is loaded with hidden vegetables and is restaurant-quality delicious! It's popular with all ages, and my favorite way to serve it is paired with a grilled cheese sandwich.

INGREDIENTS

1 tablespoon olive oil

2 carrots, finely diced

1 small onion, finely diced

3 ribs celery, finely diced

4 cups low-sodium chicken broth

2 (14½-ounce) cans diced tomatoes

2 tablespoons tomato paste

1½ teaspoons dried basil

1 teaspoon dried oregano

8 tablespoons (1 stick) unsalted butter

½ cup all-purpose flour

1½ cups half-and-half or whole milk

1 cup freshly grated Parmesan cheese

1 teaspoon salt

¼ teaspoon freshly ground black pepper

¼ cup chopped fresh basil

INSTRUCTIONS

1. Heat oil in a large soup pot over medium-high heat. Once hot, add carrots, onions, and celery and sauté for 3 minutes.

2. Add chicken broth, diced tomatoes, tomato paste, dried basil, and oregano. Bring to a gentle boil and cook for several minutes, until vegetables are tender.

3. Use a blender to puree the soup until smooth.

4. In a separate pot, prepare the roux: Melt butter over medium-low heat, then stir in the flour and whisk together, stirring for about 10 minutes or until the roux is golden brown.

5. Add a big ladleful of the soup to the roux—it will start to form a thick paste. Add a few more big scoops of soup to the roux and stir until smooth. Add the roux mixture to the soup pot and stir to combine.

6. Stir in the half-and-half, Parmesan cheese, salt, pepper, and fresh basil. Taste and add additional oregano and basil if needed. Stir well. Cook for a few more minutes until warmed through.

ALTERNATIVE COOKING METHOD

SLOW COOKER: Combine carrots, onions, celery, broth, diced tomatoes, tomato paste, basil, and oregano in the slow cooker. Cook on low for 5 to 6 hours, until flavors are blended and vegetables are soft. Blend soup, then continue with step 4 of the recipe.

Lasagna Soup

All of the flavors you love from traditional lasagna, transformed into a warm and comforting bowl of soup. This one always hits the spot.

INGREDIENTS

- ½ pound lean ground beef
- ½ pound ground Italian sausage
- ½ teaspoon salt
- ½ teaspoon freshly ground black pepper
- 1 tablespoon olive oil
- 1 yellow onion, chopped
- 3 cloves garlic, minced
- 7 cups low-sodium chicken broth
- 1 (24-ounce) jar marinara sauce (or homemade; see below)
- 2 tablespoons tomato paste
- 2 teaspoons dried parsley
- 1 teaspoon dried basil
- ½ teaspoon dried oregano
- ¼ teaspoon crushed red pepper flakes
- 9 lasagna noodles, broken into quarters, or 12 ounces of your favorite bite-size pasta
- 2 cups fresh spinach
- 10 ounces ricotta cheese
- 1 cup shredded mozzarella cheese
- ½ cup freshly grated Parmesan cheese
- Fresh chopped basil, for serving

INSTRUCTIONS

1. In a large pot over medium heat, cook ground beef and sausage, stirring to crumble into small pieces, until browned. Remove meat from the pot and set aside; discard grease.

2. Add oil to the pot and return to the heat. Add diced onion and sauté for 3 to 5 minutes. Add garlic and cook for 30 seconds. Stir in broth, marinara sauce, tomato paste, and spices. Return meat to the pot.

3. Bring to a boil, then add lasagna noodles and reduce heat to medium-low. Cook, stirring occasionally, until noodles are tender. Add spinach.

4. In a small bowl, stir together ricotta, mozzarella, and Parmesan cheeses.

5. Ladle the hot soup into bowls and add a dollop of the cheese mixture on top. Garnish with fresh basil.

LAUREN'S TIPS
MARINARA SAUCE

Try my homemade marinara found at tastesbetterfromscratch.com/marinara-sauce/.

HOW TO FREEZE

Place soup and cheese mixture in separate freezer-safe containers and freeze for up to 3 months. Thaw in the refrigerator and reheat soup on the stovetop.

Creamy White Chicken Chili

Creamy White Chicken Chili is the perfect bowl to warm up to on a cold winter day. You can make it on the stove or in a slow cooker or Instant Pot, and use leftover rotisserie chicken to make it even quicker to whip together.

INGREDIENTS

1 tablespoon olive oil

1 small yellow onion, chopped

2 cloves garlic, finely minced

2½ cups low-sodium chicken broth

2 (4-ounce) cans diced green chiles

Juice of ½ small lime

1½ teaspoons cumin

½ teaspoon dried oregano

½ teaspoon paprika

¼ teaspoon cayenne pepper

Salt and freshly ground black pepper, to taste

2 (15-ounce) cans great Northern beans, drained and rinsed

1 cup corn (frozen or fresh)

1 cup sour cream or plain Greek yogurt

2 heaping cups cooked shredded chicken

Cilantro, tortilla chips, shredded cheese, sliced green onions, and avocado slices, for topping (optional)

INSTRUCTIONS

1. Heat oil in a large pot over medium-high heat. Add onion and sauté until softened. Add garlic and cook for 30 seconds.

2. Add chicken broth, green chiles, lime juice, cumin, oregano, paprika, and cayenne, and season with salt and pepper to taste.

3. Optional: For a thicker, creamier soup, puree a big ladleful of beans and a splash of broth from the soup in a food processor until smooth.

4. Add whole beans, bean puree, if using, and corn to the soup pot. Bring the mixture to a simmer and cook, uncovered, for 15 to 30 minutes.

5. Remove from the heat and stir in sour cream and cooked chicken.

6. Serve topped with cilantro, shredded cheese, green onions, avocado slices, and tortilla chips, if using.

VARIATION

SLOW COOKER: Combine 2 raw chicken breasts with the broth, green chilies, lime juice, spices, beans, and corn in a slow cooker. (To use precooked chicken, wait to stir it in at the end). Sauté onions and garlic per step 1 and add to the slow cooker. Cook on low for 5 hours or high for 3 hours. Stir in sour cream and serve with desired toppings.

HOW TO FREEZE

Freeze soup before adding sour cream and cooked chicken. Freeze in an airtight container for up to 3 months. Thaw in the refrigerator overnight and simmer on the stovetop until warm, then stir in cooked chicken and sour cream.

LAUREN'S TIPS
CHICKEN

To use raw chicken, add 1½ pounds chopped boneless chicken in step 2, with the chicken broth.

Zuppa Toscana

A creamy Italian soup with sausage, potatoes, chopped kale, and bacon, this easy, comforting Zuppa Toscana is always a crowd favorite.

INGREDIENTS

1 pound hot ground Italian sausage

2 medium russet potatoes, peeled and chopped in ½-inch cubes

1 large onion, chopped

3 cloves garlic, minced

6 cups low-sodium chicken broth

5 slices bacon, cooked and crumbled

3 cups chopped baby kale or spinach

1 cup heavy whipping cream

Salt and freshly ground black pepper, to taste

Crushed red pepper flakes, to taste (optional)

INSTRUCTIONS

1. Chop or slice sausage into small pieces. Cook in a large soup pot over medium-high heat until browned on all sides.

2. Add potatoes, onions, and garlic and toss to combine. Pour in chicken broth and allow mixture to come to a boil.

3. Reduce the heat to medium-low and cook until potatoes are fork-tender, 8 to 10 minutes.

4. Stir in bacon, chopped kale, and cream. Season with salt and pepper and crushed red pepper flakes, if using, and cook for 2 to 3 more minutes. Serve warm.

SALADS AND SIDES

Artichoke Dip

Warm and cheesy artichoke dip is one of my favorite easy appetizers or sides. We serve it with crackers, tortilla chips, bread chunks, or chopped veggies for dipping.

INGREDIENTS

1 (8-ounce) can artichoke hearts (not marinated), drained and chopped

8 ounces cream cheese, softened

1¼ cups freshly grated Parmesan cheese, divided

½ cup sour cream

½ cup mayonnaise

1 clove garlic, minced

Fresh chopped dill or dried dill, to taste

INSTRUCTIONS

1. Preheat oven to 350°F. Grease an 8-x-8-inch or similar size baking dish or glass pie dish.

2. In a mixing bowl, combine cream cheese, 1 cup of Parmesan, the sour cream, mayo, and garlic. Mix until smooth.

3. Stir in chopped artichoke hearts and a small pinch of dill.

4. Spoon into the prepared baking dish and sprinkle remaining ¼ cup Parmesan cheese on top. Sprinkle with a little more dill to taste.

5. Bake for 20 minutes, or until hot and bubbly. Serve warm with crackers, bread, or cold veggies.

VARIATION

SPINACH-ARTICHOKE DIP: Add ½ cup frozen, thawed spinach, with the liquid squeezed out, at the same time as the artichokes.

MAKE AHEAD

Assemble 1 to 2 days ahead of time, then allow to rest at room temperature for 20 minutes before baking.

- - - - - - - - -

HOW TO FREEZE

Can be frozen before or after baking. Allow to thaw completely before baking or reheating.

Balsamic Bread Dip

Our family friend helped create this recipe in an effort to copy the balsamic bread dip from a restaurant we love. It's since been a huge hit wherever we share it—thanks for the inspiration, Chris.

INGREDIENTS

⅓ cup mayonnaise

⅓ cup Greek yogurt

3 tablespoons balsamic vinegar, or more to taste

1 tablespoon olive oil

5 cloves garlic

1 small sprig fresh rosemary, minced

Salt and freshly ground black pepper, to taste

Chunks of Easy Artisan Bread (page 68), for serving

INSTRUCTIONS

1. Combine mayo, yogurt, vinegar, oil, garlic, rosemary, and salt and pepper in a food processor and blend until smooth. Taste and adjust the seasoning as needed. Refrigerate for at least 30 minutes, if possible.

2. Serve with chunks of crusty artisan bread.

STORING LEFTOVERS

Store dip in the fridge for up to 1 week.

Guacamole

The best homemade guac is made with fresh, high-quality ingredients. It's easy and delicious.

INGREDIENTS

3 large, ripe avocados, peeled and pitted

Juice of ½ lime

1 Roma tomato, diced (optional)

⅓ cup diced red onion

¼ cup chopped fresh cilantro, or more or less to taste

½ teaspoon freshly ground sea salt, or more to taste

Pinch of cumin

INSTRUCTIONS

1. Combine avocado and lime juice in a bowl and gently mash to combine.

2. Add tomato, if using, along with onion, cilantro, salt, and cumin. Serve with tortilla chips.

VARIATIONS

SPICY: Add ½ to 1 diced jalapeño or serrano pepper. Remove seeds and ribs for milder heat.

FRUITY: Add ⅓ cup diced mango, pineapple, or pomegranate arils.

CHEESY: Add ¼ cup queso fresco, feta, or blue cheese crumbles.

LAUREN'S TIPS
USE IT UP

In addition to tortilla chips, this guac makes a great topping for Bacon Tomato Avocado Toast (page 36), Street Tacos (page 104) or Chicken Tortilla Soup (page 153).

- - - - - - - - -

STORING INSTRUCTIONS

Spoon guacamole into an airtight container and place a piece of plastic wrap directly over the surface, to keep the air from turning it brown. Secure lid and refrigerate for up to 1 week.

Homemade Salsa

This really is the best, easiest Mexican-style salsa that tastes even better than what you'd enjoy at a restaurant. The ingredients are simple and inexpensive and it only takes five minutes to make.

INGREDIENTS

1 (28-ounce) can whole peeled tomatoes, drained

2 (10-ounce) cans Rotel® diced tomatoes with green chiles

½ cup fresh cilantro

¼ cup chopped red onion

Juice of 1 lime

1 clove garlic, minced

½ teaspoon ground cumin

½ teaspoon sea salt

Pinch granulated sugar

INSTRUCTIONS

1. Combine all ingredients in a food processor and pulse a few times until no large chunks remain. Taste and adjust seasonings, if needed.

2. For best flavor, refrigerate salsa for at least 1 hour before serving.

STORING LEFTOVERS

Store in the fridge for up to 1 week. This recipe makes a little less than 6 cups of salsa. I like to fill three pint jars and share with friends and neighbors.

LAUREN'S TIPS
SPICE LEVEL

This yields a mild salsa. For more heat, use the Hot or Habanero style Rotel diced tomatoes with green chiles.

Cowboy Caviar

This chip dip is so fresh and flavorful that people just flock to it. I love how easy it is to make, using basic ingredients I usually have on hand.

INGREDIENTS

1 (15-ounce) can black beans, drained and rinsed

1 (15-ounce) can pinto beans, drained and rinsed

1 (15-ounce) can corn, drained

6 to 8 Roma tomatoes, diced

½ large sweet onion, diced

2 avocados, peeled, pitted, and diced

1 bunch fresh cilantro, finely chopped

Juice of 3 limes

Sea salt, to taste

INSTRUCTIONS

1. In a large bowl, combine beans, corn, tomatoes, and onion.

2. Gently stir in avocado and cilantro.

3. Squeeze lime juice into the bowl and add a pinch of sea salt.

4. Stir to combine. Add more sea salt to taste. Serve with tortilla chips.

Prep Time	Cook Time	Total Time	Yield
5 MINUTES	55 MINUTES	1 HOUR	SERVES 6

Baked Wedge Fries

Ultra-crispy wedge fries will satisfy your French fry craving, but are baked in the oven for a healthier take.

INGREDIENTS

- 4 large russet potatoes, scrubbed and rinsed
- ¼ cup olive oil
- 2 teaspoons garlic powder
- 1 teaspoon paprika
- 1 teaspoon salt
- ½ teaspoon freshly ground black pepper
- ½ cup finely shredded Parmesan

INSTRUCTIONS

1. Preheat the oven to 400°F. Spray a large baking sheet with nonstick cooking spray.

2. Cut each potato in half, then cut each half into 4 to 6 even-size wedges. Place potatoes on the baking sheet.

3. Whisk together olive oil, garlic powder, paprika, salt, and pepper. Drizzle over potatoes and toss to combine. Spread potatoes out on the baking sheet so they're not touching. Sprinkle with Parmesan cheese.

4. Cook for 30 minutes, then flip to the other side and cook for 20 to 30 more minutes, until golden and crisp.

Authentic Mexican Rice

I learned to make this Authentic Mexican Rice while living in Puebla, Mexico. I can confidently say it's the best, and a necessary side dish all of your favorite Mexican recipes.

INGREDIENTS

1½ cups long-grain white rice

¼ cup vegetable or canola oil

¼ cup tomato sauce, or 2 pureed tomatoes

¼ medium onion, finely diced

1 teaspoon minced garlic

3¼ cups water

1 small carrot, diced (optional)

½ cup frozen peas (optional)

3 whole serrano peppers (optional; they add flavor, but not heat)

2 teaspoons tomato bouillon granules (see note, below)

¼ teaspoon salt

LAUREN'S TIPS
TOMATO BOUILLON

This can be found in the Mexican food aisle at Walmart or your local grocery store, or online. You can substitute chicken bouillon, but the rice won't have as rich of an orange color.

INSTRUCTIONS

1. Rinse rice in a fine-mesh strainer until the water runs clear. Set aside.

2. In a large saucepan over medium-high heat, add oil. Once hot, add rice and stir to combine. Cook over medium heat, stirring frequently, until rice is lightly golden brown all over (about 10 minutes).

3. Add tomato sauce, onion, and garlic and stir. Add water and carrots, peas, and serrano peppers, if using. Add tomato bouillon and salt.

4. Bring to a boil, then cover, reduce the heat to low, and cook for about 20 minutes, or until the water is completely absorbed. Remove from the heat and allow to rest, covered, for 10 minutes before fluffing with a fork.

ALTERNATE COOKING METHODS

INSTANT POT MEXICAN RICE: Rinse rice, then cook in oil on the sauté setting until golden. Add tomato sauce, onion, garlic, water, carrots, peppers, tomato bouillon, and salt (do not add peas yet). Cook on manual/high pressure for 4 minutes with a 10-minute natural release. Remove the lid and add peas. Cover and let rest for 5 minutes, then fluff rice with a fork.

Prep Time	Cook Time	Total Time	Yield
15 MINUTES	NONE	15 MINUTES	SERVES 4 TO 6

Mushroom Bacon Swiss Salad

This spinach salad is one of my favorite family recipes. Fresh greens, mushrooms, warm crumbled bacon, cottage cheese, and Swiss cheese come together for a flavorful and unique salad that's sure to impress. The poppyseed dressing is the perfect sweet addition.

INGREDIENTS

3 cups baby spinach leaves

2 cups chopped romaine or red leaf lettuce

8 ounces white button mushrooms, sliced

½ cup freshly grated Swiss cheese

½ cup small-curd cottage cheese, rinsed and drained well

5 slices bacon, cooked and crumbled

¼ cup thinly sliced red onion

POPPYSEED DRESSING

½ cup vegetable or canola oil

¼ cup red wine vinegar or tarragon vinegar

2 tablespoons granulated sugar

2 tablespoons chopped red onion

Salt and freshly ground black pepper, to taste

½ tablespoon poppy seeds

1 teaspoon Dijon mustard

INSTRUCTIONS

1. Combine all dressing ingredients in a blender and blend until smooth. Taste and adjust as needed: Add more vinegar if you want it tangier, more sugar if you'd like it sweeter. Refrigerate until ready to use and shake well before serving.

2. Combine spinach and lettuce in a large salad bowl. Top with all remaining salad ingredients and toss lightly to combine. Drizzle with desired amount of dressing.

Butternut Squash Salad

When the weather gets cooler, I make this salad on repeat for months. The warm roasted squash pairs so deliciously with the flavors of bacon, pecans, and cranberries.

INGREDIENTS

1½ pounds butternut squash, peeled and chopped into ¾-inch cubes (about 4 cups)

1 tablespoon olive oil

¾ teaspoon salt

½ teaspoon freshly ground black pepper

3 to 4 cups baby kale

3 to 4 cups mixed greens

6 slices bacon, cooked and crumbled

½ cup dried cranberries

½ cup chopped pecans

¼ red onion, thinly sliced

⅓ cup freshly grated Parmesan cheese

BALSAMIC VINAIGRETTE

¾ cup olive oil

¼ cup balsamic vinegar

1 tablespoon Dijon mustard

2 tablespoons honey

1 tablespoon lemon juice

Salt and freshly ground black pepper, to taste

INSTRUCTIONS

1. For the vinaigrette, whisk all ingredients together and refrigerate until ready to use.

2. Preheat the oven to 400°F. Place butternut squash on a baking sheet, drizzle with olive oil, and season with salt and pepper. Toss gently to coat, then spread into a single layer.

3. Roast for 15 to 20 minutes, tossing once during cooking, until squash is tender. Allow to cool while you prepare the rest of the salad.

4. Combine kale and spinach in a large salad bowl. Top with remaining salad ingredients. Drizzle with vinaigrette and toss to coat.

LAUREN'S TIPS

MAKE IT A MEAL

Top the salad with grilled chicken for a complete meal!

Excellent!

Italian Pasta Salad

Everyone always loves this cold pasta salad, made with a simple homemade Italian dressing and loaded with all the good stuff, like fresh mozzarella and salami. It's the perfect side for a barbecue or potluck.

INGREDIENTS

- 1 pound rotini pasta
- 8 ounces fresh mozzarella cheese pearls, or chopped mozzarella
- 8 ounces salami, chopped
- 6 ounces sliced black olives
- 1½ cups halved cherry tomatoes
- ½ red onion, diced
- ½ cup sliced pepperoncinis (optional)
- ½ cup freshly grated Parmesan cheese
- 2 tablespoons chopped fresh parsley leaves

ITALIAN DRESSING (see note, right)

- ¾ cup olive oil
- ¼ cup red wine vinegar
- 2 teaspoons dried parsley
- 2 teaspoons dried minced onion
- 2 teaspoons fresh lemon juice
- 1 teaspoon dried basil
- 1 teaspoon dried oregano
- 1 teaspoon garlic salt
- 1 teaspoon granulated sugar
- ¼ teaspoon freshly ground black pepper

INSTRUCTIONS

1. To make the salad dressing, combine all ingredients in a jar with a lid and refrigerate. Shake before using.

2. Cook pasta according to package instructions. Drain pasta and rinse with cold water. Cool completely.

3. Transfer pasta to a large bowl and pour half of the salad dressing over it. Toss to combine. Add all remaining ingredients and the rest of the dressing and toss everything to combine.

4. Cover and refrigerate for 1 hour or longer before serving.

LAUREN'S TIPS
ITALIAN DRESSING

If you don't have time to make your own dressing, you can substitute 1¼ cups bottled zesty Italian dressing.

MAKE AHEAD

The dressing can be made up to 2 weeks ahead and stored in the refrigerator. Shake before using. The pasta salad can be assembled 2 to 3 days in advance and stored in the refrigerator.

Prep Time	Cook Time	Total Time	Yield
10 MINUTES	10 MINUTES	20 MINUTES	16 CUPS

Teriyaki Pasta Salad

My family has been making this salad for decades; it's just that good! I love the crunch from the water chestnuts and peanuts, and the sweetness from the dried cranberries and mandarin oranges.

INGREDIENTS

16 ounces farfalle pasta

1 pound baby spinach leaves

2 cups cooked, chopped chicken

1 (11-ounce) can mandarin oranges

1 (5-ounce) can water chestnuts, drained and chopped

½ cup dry-roasted peanuts

½ cup dried cranberries

2 tablespoons chopped sweet onion

DRESSING

½ cup teriyaki sauce (see note, below)

¼ cup vegetable or canola oil

¼ cup rice wine vinegar

INSTRUCTIONS

1. Prepare the dressing by combining all the ingredients. Set aside.

2. Cook pasta according to package directions until al dente. Rinse and drain pasta and transfer to a large bowl.

3. Toss pasta with half of the teriyaki dressing and refrigerate until cooled.

4. Add the spinach, cooked chicken, mandarin oranges, water chestnuts, peanuts, dried cranberries, and onion. Stir in remaining dressing to taste and toss to combine.

LAUREN'S TIPS

Teriyaki Sauce: My favorite is Mr. Yoshida's brand, but any good quality, thicker teriyaki sauce will work. You can also make it from scratch—visit tastesbetterfromscratch.com /teriyaki-sauce/ for my recipe.

Macaroni Salad

There's a reason macaroni salad is so popular at potlucks and barbecues, and I think my version is a total winner! It has my favorite add-ins like celery, onion, bell pepper, and shredded carrot, tossed in a creamy dressing.

INGREDIENTS

½ pound elbow or ditalini pasta

1 rib celery, diced

½ red bell pepper, diced

¼ cup shredded carrot, loosely measured, then squeezed out

¼ cup diced red onion

DRESSING

½ cup mayonnaise

¼ cup sour cream or plain Greek yogurt

2 tablespoons milk

2 tablespoons cider vinegar

½ tablespoon granulated sugar

½ tablespoon Dijon mustard

½ teaspoon salt

¼ teaspoon freshly ground black pepper

INSTRUCTIONS

1. Bring a large pot of salted water to a boil. Cook pasta according to package directions until al dente. Drain and rinse with cold water. Cool completely.

2. In a large mixing bowl, toss together pasta, celery, bell pepper, carrots, and onion.

3. In a small mixing bowl, whisk together all ingredients for the dressing.

4. Pour half the dressing over pasta and toss to coat. Cover macaroni salad and remaining dressing and refrigerate both for at least 1 hour. Stir in additional dressing just before serving (add a splash of milk for a thinner dressing, if desired).

MAKE AHEAD

Assemble the salad ingredients and the dressing through step 3 and store separately in the refrigerator for 3 to 5 days.

- - - - - - - -

STORING LEFTOVERS

Leftovers will keep in the fridge for 3 to 5 days.

Baked Potato Salad

You're guaranteed a potluck favorite with this easy Baked Potato Salad. It's a fun change from traditional potato salad, featuring all the toppings and flavors you love from a loaded baked potato, including bacon, onions, sour cream, and cheese.

INGREDIENTS

2 pounds russet potatoes
   (5 to 6 medium potatoes)

Salt and freshly ground black
   pepper, to taste

1 cup sour cream

1 cup mayonnaise

8 slices bacon, cooked and
   chopped

5 green onions, chopped

1 cup shredded cheddar cheese

INSTRUCTIONS

1. Preheat the oven to 400°F. Wash potatoes and prick them with a fork or knife.

2. Bake for 50 minutes to 1 hour, or until they are fork-tender. Remove from the oven and cool completely.

3. Peel all the potatoes, or leave half of them with skin on and peel the rest. Cut potatoes into small pieces and place in a large serving bowl. Season with salt and pepper.

4. Combine sour cream and mayonnaise in a bowl and stir well. Pour sauce over potatoes and gently stir to coat.

5. Add most of the bacon, green onions and cheese, reserving some for topping, and gently stir to combine.

6. Garnish with reserved bacon, green onions, and cheese before serving.

Gourmet Mac and Cheese

Bacon, two kinds of cheese, and a toasted panko breadcrumb topping make this baked mac and cheese gourmet both in looks and in taste.

INGREDIENTS

½ pound elbow macaroni

6 slices bacon, chopped

1 tablespoon unsalted butter

2 tablespoons all-purpose flour

1½ cups milk

¾ cup half-and-half

1½ teaspoons cornstarch

½ teaspoon Dijon mustard

1½ teaspoons Better than Bouillon® chicken base or bouillon granules

½ teaspoon onion powder

½ teaspoon garlic powder

½ teaspoon dried parsley

Salt and freshly ground black pepper, to taste

2 cups freshly grated sharp cheddar cheese

½ cup freshly grated Parmesan cheese

CRUMB TOPPING

⅓ cup panko breadcrumbs

1 tablespoon unsalted butter, melted

½ tablespoon olive oil

INSTRUCTIONS

1. Cook pasta according to package instructions just until al dente. Drain and rinse with cold water. Set aside.

2. Preheat the oven to 350°F. Lightly grease an 8-x-8-inch baking dish.

3. Cook bacon in a large skillet over medium heat until crispy. Remove to a plate lined with paper towels and wipe out some of the grease from the pan.

4. Add butter to the pan and whisk in flour. Cook, stirring, for 2 minutes. Reduce heat to low and gradually whisk in milk.

5. Combine half-and-half and cornstarch and whisk until smooth. Gradually add cornstarch mixture to the skillet followed by mustard, chicken base, onion powder, garlic powder, parsley, and salt and pepper.

6. Cook sauce for a few more minutes, just until it begins to slightly thicken. Remove from the heat and stir in cheddar cheese. Add cooked pasta and toss to combine.

7. Pour mixture into the prepared baking dish. Sprinkle Parmesan cheese on top.

8. Combine panko, melted butter, and olive oil in a skillet and cook over medium-high heat, stirring constantly, until golden brown.

9. Evenly sprinkle crumbs over the mac and cheese. Add bacon crumbles on top.

10. Bake for 20 minutes, or until hot and bubbly. Serve warm.

MAKE AHEAD

Make the sauce and cook the pasta up to 3 days ahead and store them separately in the fridge. When ready to bake, warm the sauce, add the pasta, and bake as directed.

HOW TO FREEZE

Assemble the dish through step 9, then cover well and freeze for up to 3 months. Thaw overnight in the refrigerator and bake until warmed through and the cheese is bubbly on top.

DESSERT

Chocolate Brownies

My mom's delicious, thick and Chewy Chocolate Brownies are made in one bowl, with basic ingredients. Enjoy them plain, with a sprinkle of powdered sugar, or with chocolate frosting on top.

BROWNIES

2 cups granulated sugar

1 cup canola or vegetable oil

4 large eggs

6 tablespoons unsweetened cocoa powder

1½ cups all-purpose flour

1 teaspoon salt

1 tablespoon vanilla extract

CHOCOLATE FROSTING (optional)

8 tablespoons (1 stick) unsalted butter, room temperature

½ cup unsweetened cocoa powder

Pinch of salt

1 teaspoon vanilla extract

2 to 3 cups powdered sugar

5 to 6 tablespoons milk

INSTRUCTIONS

1. Preheat the oven to 350°F. Grease a 9-x-13-inch baking pan.

2. In a mixing bowl, combine sugar and oil and stir to mix.

3. Add eggs one at a time, mixing well after each egg is added.

4. Add cocoa powder and mix. Add flour, salt, and vanilla and stir until combined.

5. Pour batter into the prepared pan and spread into an even layer.

6. Bake for 30 minutes, or until a toothpick inserted in the center comes out clean. Allow to cool completely before frosting.

FROSTING

1. Use an electric mixer to beat butter until light and fluffy.

2. Add cocoa powder and salt and mix well. Add vanilla.

3. Alternate adding powdered sugar and milk, mixing well until you reach your desired frosting consistency. Add more milk for softer frosting, or more powdered sugar for firmer frosting. Spread frosting onto cooled brownies.

HOW TO FREEZE

Freeze unfrosted or frosted brownies in an airtight container for up to 3 months. Thaw completely before serving.

Banana Bread Bars

These delicious bars may be my favorite way to use overripe bananas. They're topped with a brown butter frosting that makes for the best flavor combination.

BANANA BREAD BARS

1½ cups granulated sugar

8 tablespoons (1 stick) unsalted butter, softened

1 cup plain Greek yogurt or sour cream

2 large eggs

3 to 4 ripe bananas, mashed

2 teaspoons vanilla extract

2 cups all-purpose flour

1 teaspoon baking soda

¾ teaspoon salt

BROWN BUTTER FROSTING

4 tablespoons (½ stick) unsalted butter

2 cups powdered sugar

1 teaspoon vanilla extract

1 to 2 tablespoons milk

MAKE AHEAD

Bake and frost 1 to 2 days ahead of time. Store in an airtight container in the refrigerator.

- - - - - - - - -

HOW TO FREEZE

Bake in a disposable baking pan. Once cool, cover with aluminum foil and freeze for up to 3 months. Thaw completely before cutting and serving.

INSTRUCTIONS

1. Preheat the oven to 375°F. Grease a 9-x-13-inch pan with nonstick cooking spray.

2. Combine sugar and butter in a large bowl and beat with an electric mixer until creamed together. Mix in yogurt, eggs, bananas, and vanilla.

3. Add flour, baking soda, and salt and mix just until moistened.

4. Spread batter evenly into the prepared pan and bake for 23 to 28 minutes, or until a toothpick inserted in the center comes out clean or with a few moist crumbs. Meanwhile, make the frosting.

FROSTING

1. Heat butter in a large skillet over medium heat. Allow it to come to a simmer and cook just until it starts to turn a delicate brown and has a nutty aroma. (Watch carefully so you don't burn the butter.) Remove from the heat immediately.

2. Whisk in powdered sugar, vanilla, and 1 tablespoon milk until smooth. Add a little more powdered sugar or milk if needed to thicken or thin the frosting. Pour warm frosting over the warm bars. Allow to rest for at least 10 minutes before serving.

VARIATIONS

NUTS OR CHOCOLATE CHIPS: Add ⅔ chopped walnuts, pecans, or chocolate chips to the batter before baking.

CREAM CHEESE FROSTING: A cream cheese frosting in place of the brown butter frosting would also be delicious. Visit tastesbetterfromscratch.com/cream-cheese-frosting/ for my recipe.

Peanut Butter Bars

These ultra-thick, soft, and chewy Peanut Butter Bars are made extra chewy from oats, and layered with creamy peanut butter and a rich chocolate glaze.

BARS

12 tablespoons (1½ sticks) unsalted butter

1 cup packed light brown sugar

½ cup granulated sugar

2 large eggs

½ cup creamy peanut butter, plus more for topping

½ teaspoon vanilla extract

2 cups old-fashioned rolled oats

1½ cups all-purpose flour

2½ teaspoons baking soda

½ teaspoon salt

CHOCOLATE FROSTING

4 tablespoons (½ stick) unsalted butter

1 tablespoon unsweetened cocoa powder

1¼ cups powdered sugar

1½ tablespoons milk

1 teaspoon vanilla extract

BARS

1. Preheat the oven to 350°F. Grease a 9-x-13-inch baking pan.

2. In a large mixing bowl, cream together butter, brown sugar, and granulated sugar.

3. Add eggs, peanut butter, and vanilla and mix well.

4. In a separate bowl, mix together oats, flour, baking soda, and salt, then add dry mixture to the wet ingredients.

5. Press firmly into the prepared pan. Bake for 17 to 21 minutes, or until bars look set and no longer jiggle in the center. They will harden as they cool. Allow to cool completely.

6. Once cooled, spread a thin layer of peanut butter over the bars.

FROSTING

1. Heat butter in a small saucepan over medium heat. Once melted, stir in cocoa powder.

2. Remove from the heat and add powdered sugar, milk, and vanilla. Whisk until smooth. (Or use an electric mixer to get out any lumps, if needed.)

3. Spread chocolate frosting over the top of the bars. Allow to set for 20 minutes, then cut into rectangles and serve.

Prep Time	Cook Time	Total Time	Yield
10 MINUTES	30 MINUTES	40 MINUTES	15 BARS

S'mores Bars

No campfire required for these gooey, chewy S'mores Bars, made with a graham cracker cookie base and topped with chocolate and marshmallow creme.

INGREDIENTS

2 cups all-purpose flour

2 cups graham cracker crumbs

1 teaspoon baking powder

¼ teaspoon salt

16 tablespoons (2 sticks) unsalted butter, softened

1½ cups packed light brown sugar

2 large eggs

1 teaspoon vanilla extract

7 ounces marshmallow creme (see note, below)

3 (4.4-ounce) Hershey's chocolate bars, or 2½ cups chocolate chips

INSTRUCTIONS

1. Preheat the oven to 350°F. Line a 9-x-13-inch pan with parchment paper.

2. In a medium bowl, combine flour, graham cracker crumbs, baking powder, and salt.

3. In a separate large bowl, cream butter and brown sugar together until light and fluffy, about 2 minutes. Add the eggs and vanilla and mix. Reduce the mixer speed to low and add flour mixture, mixing until combined.

4. Press half of the dough mixture evenly into the bottom of the prepared pan.

5. Dollop marshmallow creme on top and gently spread into an even layer.

6. Break chocolate bars into pieces and layer over the marshmallow. Dollop the remaining dough over the chocolate and spread out the best you can.

7. Bake for 28 to 32 minutes, or until golden brown. Allow to cool completely before cutting and serving.

LAUREN'S TIPS

MARSHMALLOW CREME

Don't substitute regular marshmallows, as they will melt and dissolve while baking.

- - - - - - - - -

HOW TO FREEZE

Wrap bars tightly in plastic wrap, then place in an airtight, freezer-safe container and freeze for up to 3 months.

Prep Time 40 MINUTES	**Cook Time** 10 MINUTES	**Total Time** 50 MINUTES	**Yield** 2 DOZEN

Peanut Butter Blossoms

Soft and chewy peanut butter cookies with a Hershey's kiss in the center. They taste as great as they look.

INGREDIENTS

24 Hershey's® chocolate kisses

8 tablespoons (1 stick) unsalted butter

½ cup creamy peanut butter

¾ cup granulated sugar, divided

½ cup packed light brown sugar

2 large eggs

½ teaspoon vanilla extract

1⅔ cups all-purpose flour

1 teaspoon baking soda

¼ teaspoon salt

INSTRUCTIONS

1. Place chocolate kisses in the refrigerator or freezer to chill.

2. In a mixing bowl, cream together butter, peanut butter, ½ cup granulated sugar, and the brown sugar until light and fluffy, about 2 minutes.

3. Add eggs, mixing after each addition. Mix in vanilla.

4. In a separate bowl, whisk together flour, baking soda, and salt.

5. Stir dry ingredients into the wet ingredients and mix gently to combine. The dough will be soft. Cover and refrigerate for 30 minutes.

6. Preheat the oven to 375°F. Pour remaining ¼ cup granulated sugar into a small bowl. Line a cookie sheet with parchment paper.

7. Scoop dough into tablespoon-size balls and roll each in sugar before placing on prepared cookie sheet.

8. Bake for 9 to 12 minutes, just until set. They will be pale and the tops will begin to slightly crack, and will look just barely set. They will firm up as they cool.

9. Remove from the oven and cool on the baking sheet for 2 to 3 minutes. Press a chilled Hershey's kiss in the center of each cookie and transfer to a cooling rack to cool completely.

MAKE AHEAD

These taste great made one day ahead of time, or you could make the dough and store it in the refrigerator for 1 day before rolling in sugar and baking.

- - - - - - - - -

HOW TO FREEZE

Freeze cookie dough or baked cookies in an airtight container for up to 3 months. Thaw dough before baking or bake from frozen, adding a few minutes to the bake time.

STORING LEFTOVERS

Store cookies at room temperature in an airtight container for up to 1 week.

Chocolate Chip Cookies

Soft and chewy on the inside with a little crisp on the outside, these are truly perfect Chocolate Chip Cookies.

INGREDIENTS

12 tablespoons (1½ sticks) unsalted butter

1 cup packed light brown sugar

½ cup granulated sugar

1 large egg + 1 egg yolk

2 teaspoons vanilla extract

2 cups + 2 tablespoons all-purpose flour

½ teaspoon baking soda

½ teaspoon salt

1½ cups semisweet or milk chocolate chips

HOW TO FREEZE

Freeze cookie dough or baked cookies in an airtight container for up to 3 months. Thaw dough before baking or bake from frozen, adding a few minutes to the bake time.

INSTRUCTIONS

1. Melt butter for 45 seconds in the microwave, until it's almost completely melted. Remove and stir, allowing any remaining butter to melt. Allow butter to cool until it's almost room temperature, but still a liquid.

2. Transfer melted butter to a mixing bowl, add both sugars, and mix until well combined. Add egg, egg yolk, and vanilla and stir until combined.

3. In a medium bowl, mix together flour, baking soda, and salt.

4. Stir dry ingredients into the wet ingredients and begin to mix. Add chocolate chips, stirring just until combined. Refrigerate dough for at least 30 minutes or up to 2 days.

5. Preheat the oven to 350°F. Line a cookie sheet with parchment paper.

6. Scoop dough into 18 balls. Bake in batches on the prepared cookie sheet for 10 to 12 minutes, or until set on top. Cool for 10 to 15 minutes on the cookie sheet before moving to a wire cooling rack.

VARIATION

SKILLET COOKIE: Press dough into a 10- to 12-inch cast iron skillet. Bake for 28 to 35 minutes, or until barely golden. Cool for 20 minutes before cutting and serving warm, with ice cream.

Rolo Cookies

Big and chewy chocolate cookies with a warm chocolate and caramel Rolo surprise baked inside.

INGREDIENTS

1½ cups all-purpose flour

½ cup cocoa powder

½ teaspoon baking powder

½ teaspoon baking soda

¼ teaspoon salt

12 tablespoons (1½ sticks) unsalted
butter, softened

½ cup + 2 tablespoons granulated
sugar, divided

¾ cups packed light brown sugar

1 egg, room temperature

1 teaspoon vanilla extract

12 Rolo candies, unwrapped

MAKE AHEAD

Dough can be made up to
3 days ahead and stored in
an airtight container in the
refrigerator.

- - - - - - - - -

HOW TO FREEZE

Freeze cookie dough or
baked cookies in a freezer-
safe container for up to
3 months. Thaw dough before
baking or bake from frozen,
adding a few minutes to the
bake time.

INSTRUCTIONS

1. Combine flour, cocoa powder, baking powder, baking soda, and salt
   in a medium bowl. Set aside.

2. In another mixing bowl, combine butter, ½ cup granulated sugar, and
   the brown sugar and beat for a few minutes until creamed together.
   Add egg and vanilla and mix until combined.

3. Gradually stir in flour mixture until combined.

4. Cover bowl and refrigerate dough for at least 30 minutes.

5. Preheat the oven to 375°F. Line a cookie sheet with parchment paper.

6. Scoop 3-tablespoon-size balls of dough. Press a Rolo in the center
   of each ball and close the dough around it, rolling it to form a ball.
   Roll each ball in remaining 2 tablespoons granulated sugar and place
   on the baking sheet 2 inches apart.

7. Bake for 12 to 15 minutes, or until set around the edges (don't
   overbake).

8. Allow to cool for several minutes on the baking sheet before
   transferring to a wire rack to cool completely.

Snickerdoodles

This is my favorite snickerdoodle recipe and yields super soft and chewy cinnamon-sugar cookies.

INGREDIENTS

8 tablespoons (1 stick) unsalted butter, softened

½ cup vegetable shortening

1¾ cups granulated sugar, divided

2 large eggs

2 teaspoons vanilla extract

2¾ cups all-purpose flour

2 teaspoons cream of tartar

1 teaspoon baking soda

¼ teaspoon salt

1 tablespoon ground cinnamon

INSTRUCTIONS

1. Preheat the oven to 375° F. Line two baking sheets with parchment paper.

2. Cream together butter, shortening, and 1½ cups sugar. Add eggs and vanilla and mix well.

3. Add flour, cream of tartar, baking soda, and salt and stir until combined.

4. Roll 24 dough balls. I like to put one finished tray of rolled cookies in the fridge while I'm rolling the second, so they're easier to handle.

5. Mix cinnamon and remaining ¼ cup sugar in a bowl and roll each dough ball in it. Place cookies 2 inches apart on a baking sheet.

6. Bake for 8 to 10 minutes, or just until set. They will harden as they cool. Transfer cookies to a cooling rack to cool completely.

STORING LEFTOVERS

Store in an airtight container at room temperature for 2 to 3 days.

- - - - - - - - -

HOW TO FREEZE

Cookie dough balls can be frozen for up to 3 months. Thaw before baking or bake from frozen, adding a few minutes to the bake time. To freeze baked cookies, allow them to cool completely and place them in a freezer bag or airtight container for up to 3 months.

Pumpkin Cookies

This family recipe has been tried and tested hundreds of times, and makes perfect cakey Pumpkin Cookies. They are easily my favorite fall cookie, and better than you'd find at a bakery.

INGREDIENTS

1 cup granulated sugar

½ cup vegetable or canola oil

1 cup canned pumpkin puree

1 large egg

1 teaspoon milk

1 teaspoon vanilla extract

2 cups all-purpose flour

2 teaspoons baking powder

1 teaspoon baking soda

1½ teaspoons ground cinnamon

½ teaspoon salt

1½ cups semisweet or milk
chocolate chips

INSTRUCTIONS

1. Preheat the oven to 375°F. Line a cookie sheet with parchment paper.

2. Combine sugar and oil in a mixing bowl and stir well to mix. Add pumpkin, egg, milk, and vanilla and mix until smooth.

3. In a separate bowl, stir together flour, baking powder, baking soda, cinnamon, and salt.

4. Add dry ingredients and chocolate chips to the wet ingredients and stir just until incorporated.

5. Drop by large spoonfuls onto the prepared baking sheet. Bake for 10 to 12 minutes. Cool for a few minutes on the baking sheet, then transfer to a cooling rack.

HOW TO FREEZE

Baked cookies will keep best stored in an airtight container in the freezer for up to 3 months.

Sugar Cookies

If you like sugar cookies that are thick and super soft and chewy, this is the recipe for you. Top them with smooth cream cheese frosting.

INGREDIENTS

1 cup granulated sugar

⅔ cup vegetable shortening (or use half butter, half shortening)

2 large eggs

⅓ cup milk

1 teaspoon vanilla extract

¼ teaspoon almond extract

3 cups all-purpose flour

2 teaspoons baking powder

1 teaspoon salt

CREAM CHEESE FROSTING

8 ounces cream cheese, softened

8 tablespoons (1 stick) unsalted butter, softened

1 teaspoon vanilla extract

3 to 4 cups powdered sugar

HOW TO FREEZE

Freeze sugar cookies with or without frosting for up to 3 months. If frosted, freeze them in a single layer for 30 minutes, then transfer to an airtight container with parchment paper between the stacked layers and return to the freezer. The cookie dough can also be frozen for up to 3 months. When ready to bake the cookies, remove the dough from the freezer about 1 hour ahead of time to allow it to come to room temperature before rolling it out.

INSTRUCTIONS

1. In a mixing bowl, cream together sugar and shortening. Add eggs, milk, and vanilla and almond extracts and mix.

2. In a separate bowl, mix flour, baking powder, and salt. Add to the wet ingredients and mix until you form a large dough ball. Refrigerate for 30 minutes.

3. Preheat the oven to 350°F. Line a baking sheet with parchment paper.

4. Lightly flour your countertop. Place dough on the floured surface and use a rolling pin to roll out to ½ inch to ¾ inch thick.

5. Cut the dough into shapes with cookie cutters and place cookies on the prepared baking sheet.

6. Bake for 7 to 10 minutes. Cookies will be very light colored and just set when you take them out. They will harden as they cool, so don't overbake them. Cool on the baking sheet for a few minutes before transferring to a rack to cool.

FROSTING

1. Combine cream cheese and butter in a mixing bowl and beat well until smooth and creamy.

2. Add vanilla. Add powdered sugar, starting with 3 cups and adding more as needed until the frosting is smooth and thick. Allow cookies to cool completely before frosting.

Prep Time 15 MINUTES	**Cook Time** 35 MINUTES	**Total Time** 50 MINUTES	**Yield** ABOUT 6 CUPS

Excellent!

Apple Crisp

Thinly sliced tart apples baked with a cinnamon glaze and oatmeal crumb topping make this recipe a must-try. It has hundreds of rave reviews on the website.

CRUMB TOPPING

8 tablespoons (1 stick) unsalted butter, cut into small pieces

⅔ cup rolled oats

½ cup all-purpose flour

½ cup packed light brown sugar

½ teaspoon baking powder

½ teaspoon ground cinnamon

Pinch of salt

APPLE FILLING

3 tablespoons butter, melted

2 tablespoons all-purpose flour

3 tablespoons milk

1 tablespoon lemon juice

½ teaspoon vanilla extract

¼ cup packed light brown sugar

½ teaspoon ground cinnamon

⅛ teaspoon ground nutmeg

3 to 4 large Granny Smith *Honeycrisp* apples, peeled, cored, and thinly sliced

FOR SERVING (optional)

Vanilla ice cream

INSTRUCTIONS

1. Preheat the oven to 375°F and grease an 8-x-8-inch or similar size baking dish.

2. In a medium bowl, combine all crumb topping ingredients and mix with a fork or pastry blender until well combined. Refrigerate while you prepare the apple filling.

3. In a small bowl, stir together melted butter and flour. Add milk, lemon juice, and vanilla and stir well. Stir in brown sugar, cinnamon, and nutmeg.

4. Pour butter mixture over apples and toss to coat. Pour into the prepared baking dish and spread into an even layer.

5. Sprinkle crumb topping evenly over the apples.

6. Bake for 30 to 35 minutes, or until golden brown and top is set.

7. Remove from the oven and allow to cool for at least 10 minutes before serving.

8. Serve with vanilla ice cream, if desired.

RECIPE ADAPTED FROM COOKINGCLASSY.COM

Peach Cobbler

This old-fashioned Peach Cobbler recipe is not only extremely easy to make from scratch, it can also be made with fresh or canned peaches so you can enjoy it all year round!

PEACHES (see note, below)

5 peaches, peeled, cored, and sliced (about 4 cups)

½ cup granulated sugar

¼ teaspoon salt

BATTER

6 tablespoons (¾ stick) unsalted butter

1 cup all-purpose flour

1 cup granulated sugar

2 teaspoons baking powder

¼ teaspoon salt

¾ cup milk

Ground cinnamon, to taste

LAUREN'S TIPS

Canned peaches: To substitute canned peaches, use a 1-quart jar, undrained. Omit the ½ cup granulated sugar and salt from step 1 and skip right to step 3.

INSTRUCTIONS

1. Combine peaches, sugar, and salt in a saucepan and stir to combine.

2. Cook over medium heat for just a few minutes, until sugar is dissolved and peaches have released their juice. Remove from the heat and set aside.

3. Preheat the oven to 350°F. Slice butter into pieces and place in a 9-x-13-inch baking dish. Place the pan in the oven while it preheats, to allow the butter to melt. Once melted, remove the pan from the oven.

4. In a large bowl, mix together flour, sugar, baking powder, and salt. Stir in milk just until combined. Pour the mixture into the pan over the melted butter and smooth it into an even layer.

5. Spoon peaches and their juice (or canned peaches, if using) over the batter. Sprinkle cinnamon generously over the top.

6. Bake for 38 to 40 minutes. Serve warm, with a scoop of ice cream if desired.

Prep Time	Cook Time	Total Time	Yield
15 MINUTES	40 MINUTES	55 MINUTES	6 CUPS

Triple Berry Pie

This Triple Berry Pie ranks in my top favorite pie recipes. It holds together perfectly when sliced, and you can use fresh or frozen berries for the filling.

INGREDIENTS

Dough for 2 pie crusts (page 225)

7 cups fresh or frozen raspberries, blueberries, and blackberries

1 cup granulated sugar, plus extra for sprinkling

1 tablespoon lemon juice

4 tablespoons cornstarch

2 tablespoons butter

1 large egg white beaten with a fork

BERRY FILLING:

1. Add berries, sugar, and lemon juice to a large saucepan over medium heat.

2. Simmer, until warm and juicy, about 5-10 minutes, gently stirring occasionally. Spoon out about ½ cup of the juice from the pan into a bowl. Stir cornstarch into the reserved juice. Pour cornstarch mixture into the pot of berries and cook until thickened, about 2-5 minutes.

3. Remove from heat and stir in butter. Allow berry filling to cool.

4. Prepare pie crusts: Roll out one disk of chilled pie dough until you have a circle 12 inches in diameter. Carefully place the dough into a 9-inch pie dish.

5. Pour berry filling into unbaked pie shell.

LATTICE TOP:

1. Roll out the second pie dough disc into a circle, 12 inches in diameter. Cut the dough into strips, at least 1 inch wide. Lay half of the strips vertically and evenly spaced on top of the filled pie. Use the longer strips in the center and the shorter strips on the ends.

2. Fold every other strip back almost off of the pie. Add an unused strip, laying perpendicular, on top. Return the strips you folded back, and repeat the process, folding back every other section, as you add a new piece, so that the strips on the pie follow an over-under pattern.

3. Fold excess dough along the edges of the pie and pinch them with the bottom pie crust, to seal the crust and create an edge. Crimp the edges of the pie, then brush with egg whites, and sprinkle with a little sugar.

4. Bake at 400°F for 40-45 minutes. Check it after about 25 minutes and place a piece of aluminum over it if the top crust is getting too brown.

5. Remove to a wire cooling rack and allow to cool for several hours. Store covered in the fridge.

MAKE AHEAD

Prepare pie completely 1-2 days ahead of time and store covered in the fridge. The berry pie filling can also be prepared a few days ahead of time and stored in the fridge.

HOW TO FREEZE

Baked and cooled pie can be frozen for up to 3 months. Thaw overnight in the refrigerator and allow to come to room temperature before serving.

Blueberry Sour Cream Pie

I wanted to recreate one of our favorite pies from a bakery in southern Utah, and after a bit of trial and error, I'm so thrilled with the result! I'll be making this fantastic pie for years to come.

INGREDIENTS

1 (9-inch) baked Perfect Pie Crust (page 225)

BLUEBERRY LAYER

3 cups frozen wild blueberries (or 2 cups regular frozen blueberries), divided

¼ cup + 1 teaspoon granulated sugar

2 teaspoons lemon juice

1 teaspoon cornstarch

PUDDING LAYER

1 cup granulated sugar

3½ tablespoons cornstarch

1 cup milk

Juice and zest of 1 lemon

2 large egg yolks, lightly beaten

4 tablespoons (½ stick) unsalted butter, softened

¾ cup sour cream

WHIPPED TOPPING

1 cup heavy whipping cream

2 tablespoons granulated sugar

BLUEBERRY LAYER

1. Combine 2 cups of blueberries, the sugar, and lemon juice in a saucepan over medium heat. Bring to a low boil and cook for 4 to 5 minutes.

2. Spoon out some of the juice and stir with cornstarch. Pour cornstarch slurry into the pot and cook until berry mixture is thickened, 1 to 2 minutes.

3. Stir in remaining 1 cup blueberries and remove from the heat. Allow to cool for a few minutes, then pour berry mixture into the baked and cooled pie shell.

PUDDING LAYER

1. In a large saucepan, combine sugar and cornstarch. Whisk in milk and lemon juice. Cook over medium heat, stirring constantly, until mixture is thick and bubbling. Reduce heat to low and cook for 2 more minutes.

2. Add a spoonful of the hot mixture to the egg yolks and stir well. Repeat this process with two or three more spoonfuls of the hot mixture, stirring into the egg yolks to temper them. Pour warmed egg yolk mixture into the saucepan and stir well.

3. Bring mixture to a gentle boil and cook for 2 more minutes. Remove from the heat. Stir in softened butter and lemon zest.

4. Allow the mixture to cool for a few minutes, then stir in sour cream. Pour pudding over the berry layer in the pie shell.

TOPPING

1. In a mixing bowl, beat cream with an electric mixer. While beating, add sugar. Continue beating until stiff peaks form. Spread whipped cream over pie filling.

2. Refrigerate pie for at least 3 hours before serving.

Chocolate Cream Pie

This rich and decadent pie is every chocolate lover's dream! It starts with an Oreo crust, filled with homemade chocolate pudding, topped with sweetened whipped cream.

OREO CRUST

24 whole Oreo® cookies

5 tablespoons unsalted butter, melted

CHOCOLATE PUDDING FILLING

2½ cups whole milk

⅓ cup granulated sugar

¼ teaspoon salt

6 large egg yolks

2 tablespoons cornstarch

6 tablespoons (¾ stick) unsalted butter, chopped into pieces

8 ounces good-quality semisweet chocolate, chopped

1½ teaspoons vanilla extract

WHIPPED TOPPING

1 cup heavy whipping cream

2 tablespoons powdered sugar or granulated sugar

1½ teaspoons vanilla extract

Chocolate curls, for topping, if desired

CRUST

1. Preheat the oven to 350°F. Place Oreos in a food processor and pulse into fine crumbs. Pour the crumbs into a bowl and stir in melted butter.

2. Press mixture evenly and firmly into the bottom and up the sides of a 9-inch pie dish. Bake for 10 to 12 minutes. Set aside to cool.

FILLING

1. Combine milk, sugar, and salt in a medium saucepan over medium heat and whisk well to combine. Bring mixture to a simmer, whisking frequently.

2. Meanwhile, combine egg yolks and cornstarch in a bowl and whisk until smooth.

3. Once the saucepan mixture is simmering, add a few spoonfuls of the hot liquid to the egg yolks and whisk to temper the eggs. Add a few more spoonfuls of the hot liquid to the egg yolks. Then slowly whisk the egg yolk mixture back into the saucepan. Whisk constantly until the mixture begins to thicken and comes to a very gentle boil (big bubbles begin to break the surface).

4. Remove the pan from the heat and whisk in butter, chopped chocolate, and vanilla extract. Stir until completely smooth.

5. Pour filling into the cooled cookie crust and smooth into an even layer. Place a piece of plastic wrap gently on top and refrigerate until filling is set, 4 to 6 hours, or overnight, if desired.

TOPPING

1. Once pudding has set, make the topping. In a mixing bowl, mix cream with an electric mixer on high speed for 1 to 2 minutes. Add sugar and vanilla extract. Continue mixing until soft peaks form, 2 to 3 minutes.

2. Spread whipped cream over pie and top with chocolate curls or shavings, if using.

LAUREN'S TIPS
PIE CRUST

You can also use a traditional baked pie crust (page 225) or a graham cracker crust for this pie.

- - - - - - - - -

MAKE AHEAD

You can make this pie 1 to 2 days ahead of time. Store it gently covered in the refrigerator.

Perfect Pie Crust

Tender, flaky, and buttery pie crust is so easy to make from home, especially with a few little tricks.

INGREDIENTS

2½ cups all-purpose flour

1 teaspoon salt

6 tablespoons (¾ stick) unsalted butter, frozen

¾ cup vegetable shortening, chilled

½ cup ice water

MAKE AHEAD

Pie dough can be stored in the fridge, either shaped into discs and wrapped in plastic wrap or rolled out, placed in a pie pan, and covered, for up to 3 days.

- - - - - - - - -

HOW TO FREEZE

Pie dough can be frozen for up to 3 months. To freeze, either wrap dough discs in plastic wrap, then place in a freezer bag, or roll out pie dough and place in a freezer-safe pan, wrap well in plastic wrap, and cover with aluminum foil.

INSTRUCTIONS

1. Combine flour and salt in a large mixing bowl. Grate frozen butter into the bowl. Add chilled shortening. Use a pastry blender or forks to cut the fats into the flour until the mixture resembles coarse crumbs.

2. Add ice water 1 tablespoon at a time until the dough begins to clump together into a ball. You may not need all of the water.

3. Gently mold the dough into a ball, then divide it into 2 equal pieces. Press each piece gently with your hands into a flat disk, then cover with plastic wrap and refrigerate for 2 hours, or stick in the freezer for 30 minutes.

4. To roll out pie dough, dampen a large towel or cloth and lay it flat on your countertop. Place a large piece of parchment paper over it. Lightly flour both sides of one pie dough disc and set it on the parchment paper.

5. Starting at the center of the dough, use a rolling pin to roll the pie dough out into a large circle, larger than your 9-inch pie dish. Pick up the dough from the bottom of the parchment paper and gently flip it over into the pie dish, guiding it in with your hands. Remove the parchment paper and settle the crust into the bottom and sides of the pie dish.

FOR A TWO-CRUST PIE

1. Repeat rolling with the second dough disc, and follow the recipe's instructions on filling and baking your pie.

FOR RECIPES REQUIRING A BAKED PIE CRUST

1. Preheat the oven to 375°F.

2. Trim and crimp the edges of the dough in the pan. Place a large piece of parchment paper on top of the dough and add pie weights, or 1 heaping cup of dry beans or rice, to weigh down the crust as it bakes. Bake for 15 to 20 minutes, then remove the crust from the oven and lift out parchment paper and weights. Prick the bottom of the crust all over with a fork, then return to the oven to bake for an additional 10 to 15 minutes, or until golden brown on the edges.

RECIPE WAS INSPIRED BY MY GRANDMOTHER'S RECIPE AND HTTPS://SALLYSBAKINGADDICTION.COM

German Chocolate Cake

Another treasured family recipe, my mom's German Chocolate Cake is still the most-requested birthday cake in my family. It has layers of moist chocolate cake, coconut pecan frosting, and chocolate buttercream. This cake is incredible!

CHOCOLATE CAKE

2 cups granulated sugar

1¾ cups + 2 tablespoons all-purpose flour

¾ cup unsweetened cocoa powder

1½ teaspoons baking powder

1½ teaspoons baking soda

1 teaspoon salt

2 large eggs

1 cup buttermilk

½ cup vegetable or canola oil

2 teaspoons vanilla extract

1 cup boiling water or hot coffee

COCONUT FROSTING

½ cup packed light brown sugar

½ cup granulated sugar

8 tablespoons (1 stick) unsalted butter

3 large egg yolks

¾ cup evaporated milk

1 cup chopped pecans

1 cup shredded sweetened coconut

1 tablespoon vanilla extract

CHOCOLATE FROSTING

8 tablespoons (1 stick) unsalted butter, melted

⅔ cup unsweetened cocoa powder

3 cups powdered sugar

⅓ cup milk

1 teaspoon vanilla extract

CAKE

1. Preheat the oven to 350°F. Line two 8-inch round baking pans with parchment paper and then spray lightly with nonstick cooking spray. Set aside.

2. Stir together sugar, flour, cocoa, baking powder, baking soda, and salt in a large bowl.

3. Add eggs, buttermilk, oil, and vanilla and mix until well combined.

4. Stir in boiling water. Batter will be thin, but that's okay. Pour batter into prepared pans.

5. Bake 30 to 35 minutes, or until a toothpick inserted in the center of the cake comes out clean. Cool 5 minutes in the pan, then invert onto a cooling rack to cool completely.

COCONUT FROSTING

1. In a medium saucepan, combine brown sugar, granulated sugar, butter, egg yolks, and evaporated milk. Stir to combine and bring the mixture to a low boil over medium heat. Stir constantly for several minutes, until the mixture thickens. Remove from heat and stir in pecans, coconut, and vanilla.

CHOCOLATE FROSTING

1. Combine melted butter and cocoa powder in a mixing bowl and stir to mix. Alternately add powdered sugar and milk, beating until frosting reaches spreading consistency. Stir in vanilla.

ASSEMBLY

1. Place one of the cake rounds on a serving plate. Smooth a thin layer of chocolate frosting over the cake layer, then spoon half of the coconut frosting on top, spreading it into a smooth layer. Leave about ½ inch between the filling and the edge of the cake. Stack the second cake round on top. Smooth chocolate frosting over the entire cake.

2. Spoon remaining coconut frosting on top of the cake.

MAKE AHEAD

The coconut frosting and chocolate frosting can be made several days in advance and stored in the fridge. Freeze the baked, unfrosted cakes for up to 1 month, wrapped tightly in plastic wrap. Remove frostings from the fridge 1 hour before assembling the cake to allow them to come to room temperature.

Tres Leches Cake

"Three milks" cake is a popular Mexican dessert that consists of an ultralight cake soaked in a sweet milk mixture and topped with fresh whipped cream and cinnamon.

INGREDIENTS

1 cup all-purpose flour

1½ teaspoons baking powder

¼ teaspoon salt

5 large eggs

1 cup granulated sugar, divided

⅓ cup whole milk

1 teaspoon vanilla extract

1 (14-ounce) can sweetened condensed milk

1 (12-ounce) can evaporated milk

¼ cup whole milk

WHIPPED TOPPING

1 pint heavy whipping cream

3 tablespoons granulated sugar or powdered sugar

½ teaspoon vanilla extract

Ground cinnamon, for topping

INSTRUCTIONS

1. Preheat the oven to 350°F. Lightly spray a 9-x-13-inch pan with cooking spray.

2. In a medium bowl, combine flour, baking powder, and salt. Set aside.

3. Separate egg yolks and whites into two separate bowls. Add ¾ cup sugar to the bowl with the egg yolks and mix with an electric mixer on high speed until yolks are pale yellow. Add the milk and vanilla and stir to combine.

4. Pour egg yolk mixture over the flour mixture and stir until combined.

5. Use an electric mixer to beat egg whites on high speed. Gradually add the remaining ¼ cup sugar as you mix, and continue beating until stiff peaks form.

6. Gently fold egg whites into the batter just until combined. Pour batter into the prepared pan, smoothing it into an even layer.

7. Bake for 25 to 35 minutes, or until a toothpick inserted in the center of the cake comes out clean. Remove from the oven and allow the cake to cool completely in the pan.

8. Combine sweetened condensed milk, evaporated milk, and whole milk in a small bowl. Once the cake has cooled, use a plastic fork to poke holes in the top of the cake.

9. Slowly pour milk mixture over the the top of the cake, making sure to pour near the edges and all around.

10. Refrigerate the cake for at least 1 hour or overnight to allow it to soak up the milk.

11. Just before serving, whip heavy cream, sugar, and vanilla until stiff peaks form. Smooth on the top of the cake. Sprinkle cinnamon on top. Serve with fresh sliced strawberries, if desired.

RECIPE INSPIRED BY *THE PIONEER WOMAN*.

Texas Sheet Cake

I can't think of an easier dessert for a crowd than this delicious chocolate Texas Sheet Cake. Thanks to my mother-in-law for this family-favorite recipe that's perfect for parties and potlucks.

INGREDIENTS

1 cup water

16 tablespoons (2 sticks) unsalted butter

3 tablespoons unsweetened cocoa powder

2 cups all-purpose flour

2 cups granulated sugar

1 teaspoon baking soda

½ teaspoon salt

½ cup sour cream

2 large eggs

1 teaspoon vanilla extract

CHOCOLATE ICING

8 tablespoons (1 stick) unsalted butter

¼ cup + 2 tablespoons milk

3 tablespoons unsweetened cocoa powder

3¾ cups powdered sugar, sifted

INSTRUCTIONS

1. Preheat the oven to 350°F. Grease an 18-x-13-inch baking pan.

2. Combine water, butter, and cocoa powder in a medium saucepan over medium heat. Bring mixture to a boil, then remove from the heat.

3. In a mixing bowl, combine flour, sugar, baking soda, and salt. In another small bowl, mix together sour cream, eggs, and vanilla. Add sour cream mixture to dry ingredients and mix until smooth.

4. Pour hot butter-cocoa mixture into the batter and mix until smooth.

5. Pour into the prepared pan and smooth into an even layer. Bake for 15 to 20 minutes, or until set. Meanwhile, make the icing.

ICING

1. Combine butter, milk, and cocoa powder in a saucepan over medium heat. Bring mixture to a boil.

2. Once boiling, remove from the heat and stir in sifted powdered sugar.

3. Pour warm icing over warm cake in the pan. Use a spatula to spread it evenly over the cake. Allow frosting to set for at least 10 minutes before slicing and serving.

Pineapple Upside-Down Cake

This retro cake deserves the spotlight. It's absolutely delicious, and so beautiful when inverted to showcase the caramelized pineapple and maraschino cherry design.

PINEAPPLE-CHERRY TOPPING

- 4 tablespoons (½ stick) unsalted butter, melted
- ½ cup packed light brown sugar
- 1 (20-ounce) can pineapple ring slices
- 15 to 20 maraschino cherries

CAKE

- 6 tablespoons (¾ stick) unsalted butter, room temperature
- 1 cup granulated sugar
- 2 tablespoons vegetable or canola oil
- 1 large egg, room temperature
- 1 large egg yolk, room temperature
- 1½ teaspoons vanilla extract
- 1⅓ cups all-purpose flour
- 1¼ teaspoons baking powder
- ½ teaspoon salt
- ½ cup buttermilk, room temperature

STORING LEFTOVERS

Store leftover cake in the fridge for up to 3 days. I don't recommend freezing this cake.

INSTRUCTIONS

1. Preheat the oven to 350°F.

TOPPING

2. Pour melted butter into an ungreased, round 9-x-2-inch cake pan. Sprinkle brown sugar evenly over butter.

3. Blot any excess liquid off the fruit with paper towels. Arrange 6 to 7 pineapple slices in the pan, then arrange the cherries around the pineapple. Refrigerate while you prepare the cake batter.

CAKE

4. In a large bowl, mix butter and sugar with an electric mixer until well combined. Add oil and mix.

5. Add egg and egg yolk one at a time, beating after each addition. Add vanilla and mix.

6. Stir together flour, baking powder, and salt in a medium bowl. Alternate adding flour mixture and buttermilk to the wet ingredients, stirring to combine after each addition and ending with the flour mixture.

7. Remove cake pan from the refrigerator and pour batter evenly over topping.

8. Bake for 35 to 45 minutes, or until the top of the cake has set and a toothpick inserted into the center comes out clean or with few moist crumbs.

9. Allow to cool in the pan for 20 minutes. Then run a knife along the inside edge of the pan to loosen the sides of the cake and invert onto a serving plate. Allow to cool completely on the counter before serving.

Coconut Cake with Pineapple Filling

This Coconut Cake with Pineapple Filling is somewhat of a masterpiece, with layers of soft coconut cake, pineapple filling, and smooth and creamy coconut–cream cheese frosting. It's well worth the effort.

COCONUT CAKE

2 cups all-purpose flour

1 tablespoon baking powder

1 teaspoon salt

8 tablespoons (1 stick) unsalted butter, room temperature

2 cups granulated sugar

1¼ cups unsweetened coconut milk (from a 13½-ounce can; reserve the rest for frosting)

1½ teaspoons coconut extract

5 large egg whites

PINEAPPLE FILLING

1 (20-ounce) can crushed pineapple

⅔ cup granulated sugar

2 tablespoons cornstarch

COCONUT–CREAM CHEESE FROSTING

8 tablespoons (1 stick) unsalted butter, room temperature

8 ounces cream cheese, room temperature

4 to 5 cups powdered sugar

1 to 2 tablespoons coconut milk or regular milk

1 cup shredded sweetened coconut

CAKE

1. Preheat the oven to 350°F. Line the bottoms of two 8-inch cake pans with parchment paper and spray the bottom and sides of each pan lightly with cooking spray.

2. In a mixing bowl, whisk together flour, baking powder, and salt. Set aside.

3. In a separate mixing bowl, beat butter with an electric hand mixer or stand mixer until light and fluffy. Add sugar and mix for 1 minute. Add coconut milk and coconut extract and mix.

4. Gradually add flour mixture and mix on medium speed for 2 minutes.

5. In another bowl, beat egg whites until stiff peaks form. Fold egg whites into the batter until incorporated.

6. Divide cake batter evenly between the prepared cake pans. Bake for 25 to 35 minutes, or until a toothpick inserted in the center of the cake comes out clean or with few moist crumbs.

7. Remove the pans from the oven and allow to cool for 5 minutes before inverting them onto a cooling rack to cool completely.

8. Once cakes have cooled, use a sharp serrated knife to cut each cake round in half horizontally, so that you end up with four thin cake rounds.

FILLING

1. Combine all ingredients in a medium saucepan over medium heat. Stir well and cook, stirring frequently, until mixture thickens and looks glossy, 5 to 8 minutes.

2. Pour filling into a container and place a piece of plastic wrap directly on the surface. Once cooled, cover container and refrigerate until ready to use.

continued on page 236

MAKE AHEAD

This cake tastes best after it's been in the fridge for at least 4 hours, and I think it tastes even better the next day. I like to prepare the components a few days in advance for quick assembly. The pineapple filling, cake, and frosting can all be made up to 1 week ahead and stored separately in the refrigerator.

- - - - - - - - -

HOW TO FREEZE

After cutting each cake layer in half, wrap each layer really well in plastic wrap and freeze for up to 1 month. Frozen cakes are easier to work with, and to frost. The pineapple filling and coconut frosting can also be frozen in airtight containers for up to 3 months. Allow frosting and filling to come to room temperature before using.

continued from page 234

FROSTING

1. Beat butter and cream cheese together until smooth. Add powdered sugar and a splash of coconut milk and mix until smooth and fluffy, about 3 minutes.

2. Stir in shredded coconut, saving some for sprinkling on the sides and top of the cake, if desired.

ASSEMBLY

1. Place one cake layer on a serving plate. Spread half the pineapple filling over it. Top with another cake layer, and smooth a layer of cream cheese frosting over it.

2. Top with the third cake layer. Spread remaining half of the pineapple filling over it, then add the last cake layer. Frost the sides and top of the cake with frosting and sprinkle with shredded coconut, if desired.

3. Refrigerate for at least 4 hours before serving.

RECIPE INSPIRED BY HTTPS://ABOUNTIFULKITCHEN.COM.

Caramel Popcorn

This recipe is a favorite of ours for movie night or to bring on road trips, camping trips, and boat trips. It's crispy, sweet, buttery perfection.

INGREDIENTS

8 cups popped popcorn

6 tablespoons (¾ stick) unsalted butter

1½ cups packed light brown sugar

6 tablespoons light corn syrup

¼ teaspoon salt

1 teaspoon vanilla extract

¼ teaspoon baking soda

INSTRUCTIONS

1. Preheat the oven to 200°F. Line a jelly roll pan with parchment paper.

2. Spread popcorn in an even layer on the pan and place in the oven to warm.

3. Meanwhile, melt butter in a large nonstick skillet over medium heat. Once melted, stir in brown sugar, corn syrup, and salt until smooth.

4. Bring to a boil over medium heat, stirring occasionally. As soon as the caramel starts to gently boil, cook, stirring, for just 2 minutes more.

5. Remove from the heat and stir in vanilla and baking soda. Immediately drizzle caramel over popcorn. Toss gently with a spatula until coated.

6. Bake for 45 minutes, stirring the popcorn every 15 minutes.

Fudge

Smooth and creamy chocolate fudge made with chocolate chips and marshmallows is one of my favorite easy holiday treats.

INGREDIENTS

16 tablespoons (2 sticks) unsalted butter

1¼ cups milk chocolate chips

1¼ cups semisweet chocolate chips

1 teaspoon vanilla extract

1 (12-ounce) can evaporated milk

4 cups granulated sugar

2¼ cups mini marshmallows

STORING LEFTOVERS

Cut fudge into a few large bricks, wrap them tightly in plastic wrap and then in aluminum foil, and refrigerate for up to 1 month.

- - - - - - - - -

HOW TO FREEZE

Fudge bricks can also be tightly wrapped and frozen for up to 3 months. Thaw overnight in the fridge, then let stand at room temperature for 15 minutes.

INSTRUCTIONS

1. Line a 9-x-13-inch pan with aluminum foil and grease with cooking spray. Set aside.

2. Combine butter, both types of chocolate chips, and vanilla in an extra-large heatproof mixing bowl. Set aside.

3. In a very large, heavy saucepan, combine evaporated milk, sugar, and marshmallows. Cook over medium heat, stirring frequently, until the mixture comes to a boil, then boil, stirring constantly and scraping down the sides and bottom of the pan as you stir, for about 10 minutes, until light golden brown in color and the mixture registers 235 to 240°F on a candy thermometer.

4. Pour the hot mixture into the bowl with the chocolate chips and use an electric mixer to gently combine everything until melted and smooth. Pour into the prepared pan.

5. Chill completely in the refrigerator. Once cooled, you can pull up on the edges of the foil to lift the entire slab of fudge out of the pan.

6. Cut into small squares for serving.

VARIATIONS

PEPPERMINT FUDGE: Replace vanilla with a teaspoon of peppermint extract.

ROCKY ROAD FUDGE: Just before pouring into the pan, stir in 2 cups mini marshmallows and 1 cup salted peanuts.

Salted Caramel Rice Krispies Treats

I love adding fun twists to old classics, and this recipe yields the same gooey, crispy treat you love, with a delicious caramel flavor undertone. They're irresistible!

INGREDIENTS

6⅓ cups Rice Krispies® cereal

1 (10-ounce) bag + 1 cup mini marshmallows, divided

8 tablespoons (1 stick) unsalted butter

½ cup packed dark brown sugar

¼ cup heavy whipping cream

1 tablespoon light corn syrup

1 teaspoon vanilla extract

STORING LEFTOVERS

Cut into squares and wrap each square individually in plastic wrap. Store at room temperature or in the fridge for 2 to 3 days.

- - - - - - - - -

HOW TO FREEZE

Place wrapped treats in a freezer bag and freeze them for up to 3 months.

INSTRUCTIONS

1. Combine Rice Krispies and 1 cup of mini marshmallows in a mixing bowl. Set aside.

2. In a large pot, melt butter over medium heat. Once melted, add brown sugar, whipping cream, and corn syrup.

3. Cook, stirring constantly, until mixture begins to lightly boil. Reduce the heat to medium-low and cook, stirring, for 3 to 5 minutes, until thickened and syrupy.

4. Remove from the heat and stir in remaining 10 ounces marshmallows and the vanilla.

5. Stir until the marshmallows are melted, then quickly pour over the cereal and stir well to evenly coat.

6. Press firmly into a greased 8- or 9-inch pan. Allow to cool before cutting and serving.

ACKNOWLEDGMENTS

TO JEFF: You are the most special person in my life, and I feel blessed every day to have had your love and friendship since we were kids. No one can make me laugh or ease my burdens like you do, and you are the best dad and example to our kids. You're the unsung hero behind the scenes of it all, and words can't express my love and gratitude for all you do for me and our family. Thank you for supporting me and encouraging me to chase my dreams. I love you.

TO LIZ AND JUSTIN: Liz, you have been my partner in the blog journey since the beginning, and it makes me so happy that things have come full circle over the years to have you so involved again. You push me out of my comfort zone, and no one can get it done like you do. TBFS has reached heights that were unimaginable to me because of you! Justin, your support of us both over the years has meant so much—your willingness to move your family across the country says it all!

TO MOM AND DAD: I would not be where I am today without your love and support. I'll never tire of our regular phone calls and your infinite good advice; I always hang up inspired and uplifted. Mom, this book has so much of you in it, and I cherish your "work visits" to test recipes together. You are the ultimate sous chef. Dad, TBFS wouldn't exist without your belief in me. Thank you for holding the bar high, and for teaching me by example to work hard and dream big!

TO MY SIBLINGS, CHRIS, MIKE, TYLER, ALEXANDRA, BRYCE, AND JESSICA: You've cheered me on unconditionally over the years, and I feel blessed to have such genuine love and support in my family circle. I look up to you all so much. I'm so grateful for your infinitely honest advice, and for always making me laugh.

TO THE ALLEN FAMILY, DAVE, BROOKE, CHRIS, ALISE, JENNIE, AND BROCK: Thank you for being advocates of TBFS from the beginning, and endlessly sharing my website with your neighbors and friends over the years. I appreciate your interest, love, and support, and all of the recipes of mine that you make and share.

TO STACY, MY LOYAL, TRUSTWORTHY FRIEND, WHO HAS BEEN SO SUPPORTIVE AND INVOLVED FROM THE EARLY YEARS IN SAINT LOUIS: Thank you for always bringing 100 percent to all you do. Your ability to anticipate what is needed and take care of it without being asked has made you an invaluable asset to the team.

TO ANDREA, ALI, AND KATY: I'm blessed to benefit from your talents, and I appreciate your dependability and enthusiasm in all you do behind the scenes.

TO NICOLE: I always think back to that weekend when we were randomly bunked in a room together as strangers, and I instantly bonded with you. I feel so blessed by that introduction, and to have had the chance to work with you over the past few years. Everything you touch turns to gold, and your beautiful images have transformed my brand.

TO THE TALENTED COOKS–CHRIS M., FATIMA D., KATHY G., AND TAMMY A.–WHO INSPIRED ME WHEN I WAS YOUNG: Watching you create amazing food and experiences with total joy has definitely added to my love and passion for cooking.

TO MY DESIGNER AND EDITOR: LeAnna, thank you for holding my hand through this process and transforming the images and words into the book I've been dreaming of. Christine, thank you for your attention to detail and all of your input to help turn my ramblings into a wonderful cookbook.

TO MY BLOGGING FRIENDS: I'm blessed with a network of incredible powerhouse women who inspire me daily. Thank you for being so generous with your knowledge—I'm lucky to call you coworkers and friends.

TO MY BLOG READERS, AND THE FRIENDS WHO HAVE SUPPORTED MY BLOG OVER THE YEARS: You have allowed me to transform my passion for cooking into a career that's immensely blessed my life and family. Thank you for your comments, ratings, emails, and all the support. My wish is for this book to be a reliable tool that helps you enjoy every moment cooking in your kitchen.

INDEX